KNOW YOUR CAR
AND HOW TO DRIVE

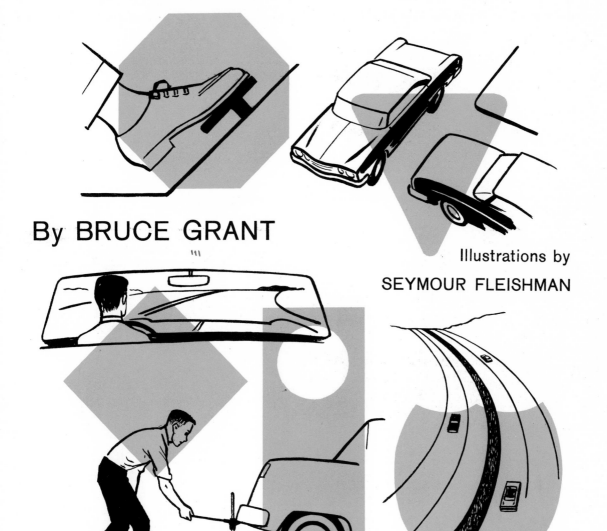

By BRUCE GRANT

Illustrations by
SEYMOUR FLEISHMAN

Hints and Tips to Stay Alive

RAND McNALLY & COMPANY   Chicago   New York   San Francisco

ACKNOWLEDGMENTS

For their assistance in reading the proofs and checking the accuracy of the text and illustrations of this book, the author wishes to express his grateful appreciation to: *Dr. Forest R. Noffsinger,* Course Development Section, Training Division, Traffic Institute, Northwestern University; *Lawton K. Smith,* Consultant in Driver Education, National Safety Council; *Richard Boyer,* Supervisor of Driver Education of Evanston Township High School; and *Charles. C. Clarke,* Assistant Manager, Insurance Information Institute.

Thanks are also due the following for their aid and suggestions in the preliminary research period: *James E. Bulger,* Vice-president, Chicago Motor Club; *Frank Burrows,* Field Director of the Citizens Traffic Safety Bureau, Chicago; *Robert A. Campbell,* Safety Co-ordinator, Illinois Division of Traffic Safety, Springfield, Illinois; *Ivan L. Eland,* Supervisor of Driver Education, Iowa State College, Cedar Falls, Iowa; *R. J. Killeen Jr.,* Service Manager, Skokie, Illinois, and *Hans H. Weinstock,* Service Representative, Chicago.

Grateful acknowledgment is also made to the following for their courtesy in supplying information and for permission to use copyrighted materials:

American Association of Motor Vehicle Administrators and the *National Safety Council* for the diagrams on pp. 16, 17, 18, 27, 29, and 46.

American Automobile Association for the diagrams on pp. 37, 41, and 43, from SPORTSMANLIKE DRIVING, 3RD EDITION, copyright by the *American Automobile Association.*

Association of Casualty and Surety Companies for the diagrams on pp. 10 and 16.

Automotive Safety Foundation and the *Institute of Traffic Engineers* for the diagram on p. 24.

Channing L. Bete Company, for the diagram on p. 48, reproduced by special permission from the Scriptographic booklet, YOU AND YOUR CAR, copyright 1957, Channing L. Bete Co., Greenfield, Mass.

Chief Justice J. Bowe and the Municipal Court of Chicago, for three diagrams on p. 17, from TRAFFIC LAWS YOU SHOULD KNOW.

Charles Carpentier, Secretary of State, Springfield, Ill., for the diagrams on pp. 10 and 35, from ILLINOIS RULES OF THE ROAD.

Ford Motor Company, for the chart on p. 11, from the booklet DEFT DRIVING; the quiz on p. 14, from the booklet NINE OUT OF TEN; and the tabular material on p. 59, from BUYERS' DIGEST OF NEW CAR FACTS FOR 1961.

General Motors Corporation, for the diagrams on pp. 38, 39, 40, 41, and 42, from POWER GOES TO WORK, copyright 1945.

Greyhound Corporation, for the diagrams on pp. 9, 18, and 28.

Household Finance Corporation, for the chart on p. 67, from MONEY MANAGEMENT, YOUR AUTOMOBILE DOLLAR.

Prentice-Hall, Inc. and *The Center for Safety Education,* New York University, for the "Driver's Code" on p. 4, reprinted from MAN AND THE MOTOR CAR, 6th ed., copyright 1959.

Rubber Manufacturers Assoc. for the diagram on p. 46.

Scott, Foresman & Company for diagrams on pp. 23 and 43, and the table on p. 21, from LET'S DRIVE RIGHT, by Maxwell Halsey, copyright 1954 by Scott, Foresman & Company.

Shell Oil Company, for the diagram on p. 21.

CONTENTS

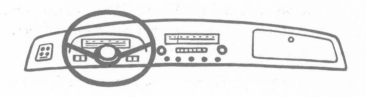

THE DRIVER'S CODE

1. I shall obey all signs, street and highway markings, signal lights, and traffic regulations.

2. I shall remember that the motor car is not a plaything, but a machine that has the power to injure and kill.

3. I shall drive at all times at a speed that is reasonable and proper under existing conditions. I shall reduce speed and observe traffic conditions carefully at all intersections, even though I may have the right of way.

4. I shall not attempt to pass other cars, unless there is plenty of room.

5. I shall give pedestrians and cyclists the right of way, even though they may be in the wrong.

6. I shall never drink any form of intoxicating liquor before driving or while a car is in my charge, nor will I ride with a driver who has been drinking.

7. I shall not attempt to drive if I am over-tired or sleepy.

8. I shall attempt to keep myself and my car in efficient operating condition at all times.

9. I shall take pride in my driving ability and constantly strive to become a better driver.

10. Realizing that "Courtesy is contagious," I will always practice the Golden Rule.

From *Man and the Motor Car, 6th Ed.* The Center for Safety Education, New York University. Copyright 1959 by Prentice-Hall, Inc., Englewood Cliffs, N.J. Reprinted by permission.

HOW GOOD A DRIVER ARE YOU?

CHAPTER **1**

HOW do you rate yourself as a driver? Of course, you have learned how to operate a car and you have passed the basic driving tests, but can you meet the standards of the real experts?

Men who drive for a living, such as cross-country bus and truck drivers, are constantly in training to keep up their driving skills. But it isn't mechanical skill alone that marks a good driver. These men have to meet strict physical and mental requirements—personality tests, too. A man at the wheel of a 20,000 pound bus has to have steady nerves, quick reactions, an even temper, and good judgment as well as physical stamina. He can't afford to "blow up" in an emergency. He has to be able to control himself as well as his car under any conditions.

Can you do the same?

BE A DEFENSIVE DRIVER

The smart driver is one who always expects the worst—who is continually on the defensive. Thus, to be a good driver, you must be a *defensive* driver. You drive always on guard to protect yourself and your car from the other driver and his car.

The defensive driver is always aware that inattention causes accidents. He keeps his eyes on the road and never "overdrives his eyes." He trains himself to judge distance accurately, and drives in such a way that he is able to stop with a safe margin of distance between his car and the car or object ahead. He keeps an eagle eye out for "problem" drivers—the showoff, the speeder, the road hog, the slowpoke—and is alert for any sudden or unpredictable actions. He takes nothing for granted.

Day or night, watch the road ahead. If you cannot see more than 25 feet ahead, slow down so that you can stop within this important 25 feet. When the road is clear and you can see a quarter of a mile ahead, regulate your speed so that you can safely stop within that distance. This goes for curves and hills, too. Keep alert to weather conditions, road conditions, and traffic conditions, and regulate your driving accordingly. All this comes under the head of defensive driving.

In fact, defensive driving covers everything that has to do with safe driving. Defensive driving means keeping your vision high and aimed well ahead; checking the road ahead for tight spots; never being lured into matching speed with other drivers; checking the rearview mirror frequently; spotting side roads; watching pedestrians; using extreme

Does overconfidence make you careless?

Do you rely too much on your past record?

Do you usually blame the other driver?

Do you take risks when you are in a hurry?

care in passing, and never driving too close to the car in front.

If practiced continuously, defensive driving will become second nature to you.

TIPS FROM T-MEN

Your personality make-up—how you think and act and feel—plays a big part in your success as a driver. The really good driver is mature in his attitude toward himself and others. He is self-confident, but not aggressive. He is courteous and considerate toward other drivers, knows and observes traffic regulations, keeps his temper under control.

Treasury agents, whose duties often require them to chase desperate criminals in high-powered cars, are carefully instructed in *driver attitudes*. In their manual on "Pursuit Driving" the T-Men are especially warned to beware of the following faulty attitudes in their driving. Do any of them apply to you?

1. Overconfidence. Taking too much for granted; assuming that a car will always perform as it should, and counting on other people to do the right thing at all times.

2. Minimizing the Seriousness of Minor Accidents. Looking upon a little bump that merely dents a fender as being of small consequence. The only way to eliminate serious accidents is to eliminate the acts that cause "little" accidents.

3. Pride in Past Record. Getting puffed up about a no-accident record. Such a driver is on the verge of a rude awakening. There are a good many people in cemeteries who, if they could talk, could honestly say, "I never had an accident until this one."

4. Faith in Experience. Believing that experience as a driver automatically makes one a good driver. However, bad habits are developed by experience as well as good ones.

5. False Ideas. Relying on guesses, estimates, legends, and fiction instead of facts. A quiz of hundreds of drivers revealed that when asked to estimate stopping distances at a given speed, 90 per cent were short more than 40 feet—a dangerous misjudgment.

DEFPO
PFTEC

*If you can read this type
at a distance of 20 feet
you have normal 20/20 vision.*

6. Self-righteousness. Judging one's own actions and usually deciding in favor of one's self—particularly in reporting accidents. Self-righteousness often causes a driver to try to punish others who, in his opinion, do something wrong in traffic.

7. Impatience. Taking needless chances just to save a little time. This results in traffic violations and, inevitably, in accidents.

HOW'S YOUR HEALTH?

Driving one of today's highly engineered cars does not require much physical strength, but it does call for alertness and quick reactions, and this means good general physical health. When you are tired, feeling "below par," your reactions are slower, your judgment is less keen, and you cannot give a top driving performance. It is best not to drive at all under such conditions, but if you must, use special care. Also, as a driver, always allow for the fact that other drivers—especially elderly people—may not be as quick or alert as you are.

Test Your Eyes. Good eyesight is an essential requirement for a good driver. In spite of all the improvements in modern cars, noth-

ing has been devised to take the place of good vision. Tinted glass, rearview mirrors, and darkened mirrors do ease eyestrain and provide wider angles of vision, but they do not compensate for poor eyesight. In fact, they actually reduce vision.

You can test your own eyesight. If you can read a line of letters ⅜ of an inch high at a distance of 20 feet, you have 20/20 vision. This is normal vision or normal visual acuity. But if at a distance of 20 feet you can just make out letters that normally can be read at 50 feet, you have 20/50 vision. In this case, and in others where vision is not normal, glasses with corrective lenses are needed.

Field of vision is another important factor in good driving. You should be able to see objects to either side of you while looking straight ahead—what Boy Scouts call having "pioneer eyes." This was an important ability for old-time scouts and woodsmen, and it is just as important for today's driver, who must be alert to everything around him.

There are several easy ways to test your field of vision. One is to hold your arms straight out at the sides at shoulder level and wiggle your thumbs while you look straight ahead. Can you see the movements of your thumbs without shifting your eyes?

A wide angle of vision is important to help you spot traffic hazards.   *The "thumb test" for field of vision.*

Another test is to stand still and look straight ahead while two persons behind you walk up to a point 20 feet to your right and left. When the one on the left comes into view you signal him to stop. Then when the right one comes into view you signal him to stop, too. If your field of vision is normal, your head should be about in line with the heads of the other two at an angle of approximately 180 degrees.

If your field of vision is narrow, you are said to have "tunnel vision." While driving you should form the habit of continually shifting your view from side to side—and drive with extreme care.

CAN YOU TRUST YOUR EYES?

Jack and Jill Went
Went Up the Hill

If you read the above two lines correctly on the first glance, it shows that you never take anything you see for granted. Many people have "anticipatory vision"—they see something familiar and jump to a conclusion which may be incorrect because they do not look carefully enough. Many traffic situations seem familiar at first glance—but look and THINK.

For instance, you may be watching the car ahead of you, and if the driver decides to beat the light you unthinkingly follow him.

Or the driver of the car ahead may be pointing out the left-hand window, or flicking the ash from a cigaret, and your "anticipatory vision" interprets this as a signal to turn left. Don't "follow the leader" blindly.

Ability to judge distance is an essential factor in driving. This is especially important when you are following another car, for then you must determine distance in relation to the speed of the other car. It is also important when passing another car with a third car approaching and in view.

A simple test to check your distance judgment is to place two automobiles facing each other, 20 feet apart and some 200 feet from where you stand to the side and rear of one of them. At your signal one car moves slowly toward the other. When you think the front bumpers of the two are in line you signal for the driver to stop. Your distance judgment should not be off more than five feet.

SLOW GLARE RECOVERY

Accidents occur three times as often per mile at night as during the day. Defective night vision and "slow glare recovery" are the causes of many night accidents. In slow glare recovery the pupils of your eyes, contracted by the glare of the headlights of an oncoming car, do not dilate or readapt themselves quickly enough after the car has passed. There may, in fact, be a few seconds of total blindness—seconds which may mean life or death. Frequently this condition is the result of a deficiency of vitamin A, and an improvement in your diet may correct it.

Avoid looking at the headlights of oncoming cars, and when you are facing such a glare, reduce your speed until you are sure your eyes have adjusted themselves. Never wear dark glasses at night. They may reduce glare, but they also reduce your vision.

The glare of approaching headlights may blind you momentarily.

TRAFFIC SIGNS AND SIGNALS

Some people are color blind. However, if you do have this defect don't let it worry you. Motor vehicle department records show few instances of accidents due to lack of color perception. With the standardization of traffic lights, with red at the top, amber in the middle, and green at the bottom, you can easily recognize the signals by their position, even if the color does not register with you. Traffic signs, too, have distinctive shapes which the good driver instantly recognizes.

Stop signs are red with white lettering, and are eight-sided. They require that the vehicle be brought to a complete stop, after which it should proceed with caution.

Caution or Reduce-speed signs are yellow with black lettering, and are diamond-shaped. They warn of such hazards as sharp curves, dangerous intersections, school zones, bridges, or hills.

Yield signs are yellow with black lettering and are triangular in shape. They always mean to yield the right of way.

Regulatory signs are usually white with black lettering and are rectangular in shape, either vertical or horizontal. The vertical signs give speed limits and other traffic regulations; the horizontal signs give instructions, such as, "Keep to the right."

Railroad Crossing signs are of two types. A circular sign with a cross is placed some distance in advance of a railroad crossing as a warning. The "crossbuck" sign is placed at the crossing. In the old days the crossbuck carried the legend: "Stop, Look, and Listen."

Traffic signals are placed at intersections as mechanical controls to regulate the flow of traffic.

The **red light** is at the top and means "stop."

The **green light** is at the bottom and gives you permission to proceed. But it means proceed with caution.

The **amber or yellow light** between the red and green is used to clear the intersection of both vehicles and pedestrians. It is a warning that the red or green light is about to change.

A single flashing yellow or amber light usu-

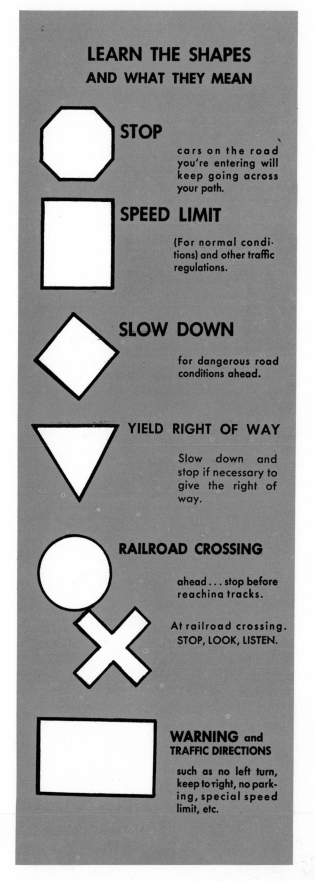

LEARN THE SHAPES
AND WHAT THEY MEAN

STOP
cars on the road you're entering will keep going across your path.

SPEED LIMIT
(For normal conditions) and other traffic regulations.

SLOW DOWN
for dangerous road conditions ahead.

YIELD RIGHT OF WAY
Slow down and stop if necessary to give the right of way.

RAILROAD CROSSING
ahead . . . stop before reaching tracks.

At railroad crossing. STOP, LOOK, LISTEN.

WARNING and TRAFFIC DIRECTIONS
such as no left turn, keep to right, no parking, special speed limit, etc.

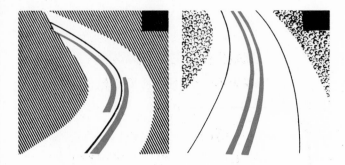

Observe all traffic lane markings.

ally marks a dangerous intersection. It means "slow down" and drive carefully. A flashing **red** light means to come to a full stop.

Arrows, lane lines, road markings and other traffic aids furnish information for the driver. Double yellow lines on hills and curves are not to be crossed under any circumstances.

LOOK OUT FOR ONE-EYED VISION

Eye fatigue is dangerous, for most people have better vision in one eye than the other, and when your eyes are tired, the better eye takes on a greater burden. The result is a type of one-eyed vision. Your ability to judge depth and distance is impaired. Try closing one eye while you try to touch something with your finger and you will realize what you are up against with one-eyed vision.

When your eyes seem tired, stop your car off the highway and rest them. Close your eyes and press your fingers lightly on the eyelids; then lift and repeat.

HOW FAR AWAY WAS THAT SOUND?

The good driver instinctively makes use of his ears as well as his eyes to judge the distance, speed, or direction of cars within his immediate vicinity. Good hearing enables you to judge the nearness of a passing car, or to locate the source of possible traffic hazards even before you can see them. Any tendency toward deafness should be corrected by a hearing aid, although this defect can be compensated for to some extent by developing increased alertness and keenness of sight.

SPLIT-SECOND ACTION

If you have a watch with a minute sweep hand, observe it carefully as you quickly say the words, "Reaction time." You will see that it takes you about half a second to pronounce these two words. This is not a test of what safety experts term a person's "reaction time," but it will indicate to you how quickly a half second goes by.

The normal driver's reaction time is a little over one half-second. It is in that split second that you see a dangerous situation ahead, receive the warning in your brain, and react to it as your brain clicks off the decision and instructs the muscles what to do.

This split second of reaction time is sufficient when a single, simple action is indicated. But if a choice of actions is necessary, your brain has to select the right one. The reaction time will then be longer—say, three-quarters of a second, or even more.

When you consider it, the short time it takes to react to a dangerous situation is amazing, yet much may happen in this split second. Suppose you are driving at 25 miles per hour, and 60 feet ahead a child suddenly darts from between two parked cars. In the

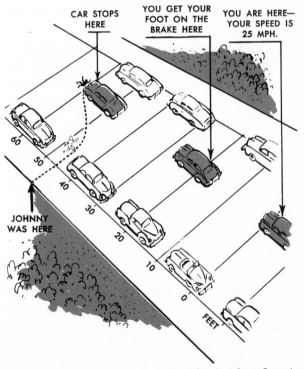

Association of Casualty & Surety Companies

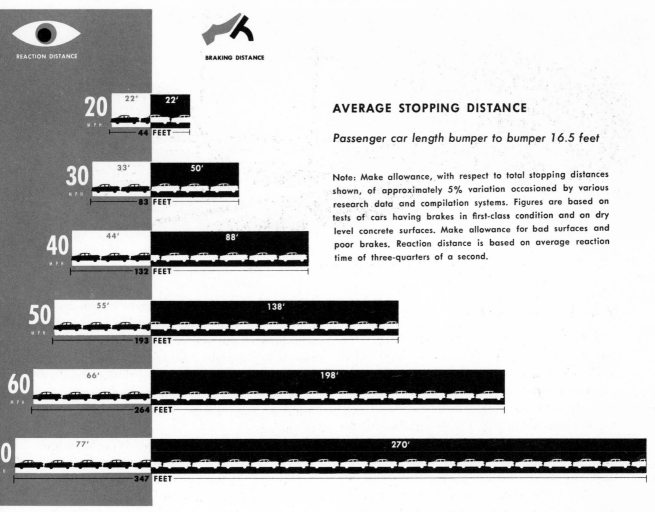

REACTION DISTANCE

BRAKING DISTANCE

AVERAGE STOPPING DISTANCE

Passenger car length bumper to bumper 16.5 feet

Note: Make allowance, with respect to total stopping distances shown, of approximately 5% variation occasioned by various research data and compilation systems. Figures are based on tests of cars having brakes in first-class condition and on dry level concrete surfaces. Make allowance for bad surfaces and poor brakes. Reaction distance is based on average reaction time of three-quarters of a second.

Ford Motor Company

split second of reaction time your car will travel 27 feet; then, even though you "jump on the brake," the car will travel another 31 feet before it stops. You will be just 2 feet from the child! If your car is traveling at 60 miles per hour, it will travel 66 feet during the instant it takes you to react. And at that speed it will travel another 200 feet before you can stop it—too late to avoid hitting the child.

As the table above shows, the distance required to bring your car to a stop increases greatly as your speed increases. At 20 miles per hour, the *total* stopping distance required (reaction time plus braking distance) is approximately 45 feet; at 50 miles per hour this jumps to 200 feet; while at 70 miles per hour you will need at least 350 feet to bring your car to a stop. This is assuming you have nor-

mal reaction time, that your brakes are in good condition, and that the pavement is dry.

No matter how quick your reflexes, no matter how good your brakes, you simply cannot "stop on a dime."

MEASURE YOUR OWN REACTION TIME

Here is a simple test to determine if you have a normal reaction time:

Hold your hand out with the fingers spread wide. Have someone hold a postcard just above the space between your thumb and forefinger. Without warning, the person drops the card and you try to catch it between your thumb and forefinger. If you miss, your reaction time is slow. If you have a slow reaction time, try to compensate for it by keeping even more alert for trouble at all times.

Highway hypnosis is one of the hazards of long-distance driving.

WATCH THAT YAWN!

Fatigue is one of the most serious driving hazards. It is especially associated with the strain of long-distance driving, but may be equally dangerous in city traffic. The man who drives back and forth to his work may be so tired at the end of the day that his reflexes are not working properly. His reaction time will slow down, and he may be incapable of judging stopping distances accurately. The smart driver will not risk his life—and those of others—by attempting to drive when he is overtired.

In turnpike or highway driving, fatigue comes on in several ways. The long drive itself may cause it. In such cases, you are aware of a growing feeling of tiredness and you can plan to stop and rest or refresh yourself before the condition becomes serious. However, on long, monotonous drives where

the car is going along at a steady high speed, there is the danger of becoming hypnotized. The hum of the motor, the drone of the tires, the long, straight, unending vista of road, may bring on a condition similar to daydreaming. You feel transported, body and mind, to a place other than behind the wheel of the car.

To overcome this insidious type of fatigue—or better still, to keep it from creeping up on you at all—move your eyes from side to side at intervals, look into the rearview mirror, at the instrument panel, and set your mind on keeping awake. Sing aloud. Turn on the radio. Vary your speed occasionally. Stop every hour or so. Eat light snacks frequently, instead of stopping for one big meal.

"TIRED ALL OVER"

Body fatigue affects not only your eyes and your mind, but your entire body and its functions. In such a case you are really "tired all over." This condition develops, on the average, after about six hours of driving—or after driving about 250 miles. It is then, when your attention is dulled and your reactions slow, that accidents may occur.

When you are alone and begin to feel tired, it is smart to pull your car off the road or into a service area and take a short nap. Even a cat nap of ten minutes or so will do wonders.

CARBON MONOXIDE

In bad weather, when it is necessary to keep the car windows closed, exhaust fumes with a dangerous concentration of carbon monoxide may seep into the car, especially if the exhaust system is not in perfect condition. Carbon monoxide has no odor and cannot be detected easily. But it will cause headache and drowsiness, and before you realize it you may fall into a deep sleep. Many an accident blamed on "falling asleep at the wheel" has been the result of carbon monoxide poisoning rather than physical fatigue. So if you cannot understand why you nod or feel drowsy while driving, have your car's exhaust system checked. It is a good idea to keep one window open just a little to let in some fresh air.

"ONE FOR THE ROAD"

Most truck drivers—and there are few better drivers behind the wheel—will not take even one beer while on duty. They know that if they should become involved in any type of accident, even though they were not at fault, they might be considered liable if they had liquor on their breath. They also know that although a drink may momentarily re-lieve fatigue, the effect will wear off in less than an hour and leave the driver in a state worse than before. A second drink, and then a third, and so on, will soon cause intoxication, and the driver's vision, reactions, and judgment will be seriously impaired. After all, alcohol is a depressant, not a stimulant.

WHEN MEDICINES ARE NOT GOOD

Although drinking drivers are responsible for a large number of all fatal auto accidents, at least liquor can usually be detected and the blame properly placed. But there are many drugs and medicines which can also impair driving performance. Antihistamines, antibiotics, anticonvulsants, benzedrine cold tablets, sedatives, even aspirin, not to speak of tranquilizers and narcotics, are often the concealed causes of driver failure.

Doctors will tell you that stimulants can cause nervousness, and so-called tranquilizers can lull a driver into such a dreamy state of well-being that his judgment is impaired.

If you are taking some form of medicine prescribed by a physician, find out from him just what effect it will have on your driving. If it is likely to bring on drowsiness, do not under any circumstances attempt to drive.

Beware of carbon monoxide fumes.

The smart driver never takes "one for the road."

Pills can be dangerous when you are driving.

HOW DO YOU REALLY RATE YOURSELF?

Always	Pts. 5
Often	3
Sometimes	1
Seldom	0

_____ I know and follow all the rules of the road.

_____ Generally drive at the same pace as the rest of traffic.

_____ Leave ample space between me and the car in front.

_____ Check the mirrors every few seconds to know what is behind.

_____ Give the other driver a break, even if the law is on my side.

_____ Signal intentions to others with tap of horn, turn indicators or lights —do it early.

_____ Expect the other driver to do the unexpected.

_____ Am aware of hazards confronting driver ahead of me.

_____ Change lanes only when clear behind and double check blind spot.

_____ Adjust speed with ability to see . . . on hills, curves, and at night.

_____ I drive only when in good physical shape.

_____ I keep my vehicle in good operating condition.

_____ Give trucks and buses extra room.

_____ I space myself between herds in traffic.

_____ Leave plenty of space around the car for seeing and stopping distance.

_____ Drive _below_ set speed limits during adverse conditions.

_____ Look ahead at least a block in town and a half mile in the country.

_____ Put lights on when needed to be _seen_ by other driver.

_____ _Look_ before pulling out into moving traffic.

_____ Have plenty of room for passing both in front and behind.

_____ Dim lights when approaching oncoming vehicles _and when following._

_____ I make smooth, unhurried stops.

Over 90	Exceptional Driver
80	Expert Driver
60	Average Driver
40	Don't Drive

Reprinted by permission of Ford Motor Company.

CHAPTER 2 CITY DRIVING

HANDLING a car in city traffic will really test your ability as a good driver. Here "defensive" driving is especially important. The numbers of moving and parked cars as well as pedestrians, the frequent traffic lights and signs, unguarded intersections, and the unpredictable actions of drivers and pedestrians make city driving a constant challenge.

You may have to make more decisions in driving an average city mile than you would in hundreds of miles on a superhighway!

POINTERS FOR CITY DRIVING

1. Regulate Your Speed. Good city driving requires that you conform to the general speed of traffic—not too fast and not too slow. Speed limits are usually well posted according to zones and should be observed.

2. Signal Your Moves. Remain in the same lane as much as possible. Other drivers expect you to keep in your lane unless you give a timely and proper warning either with your directional turn signal, or by hand signals. Certain hand signals are widely used: the hand and arm straight out to the left for a left turn; the arm bent at the elbow and the hand held straight up for a right turn; and the hand and arm turned down to indicate you are stopping. A backward or up-and-down gesture of the arm is often used to signal a warning to following cars to slow down quickly.

3. Keep To One Lane. Changing lanes is sometimes necessary, but dodging from lane to lane to "beat the traffic" is simply inviting trouble. The law terms this "weaving," and traffic policemen are on the watch for weavers as possible causers of collisions. "Tailgating"—crowding too close to the car ahead—is another dangerous practice, as it is almost impossible to avoid a collision if the car ahead stops suddenly. On the other hand, "slowpoke driving" may result in accidents by making it necessary for following cars to shift to other lanes. Collisions can be caused both by recklessness and by being overly cautious.

4. Pass Carefully. Be especially careful when passing another moving car. The general rule is to pass on the left, but there are times when traffic is moving in the same direction in two or more lanes and the right-hand lane is moving faster than the left. Then you may pass on the right. In most states a car may pass another on the right when the car ahead is preparing to make a left turn

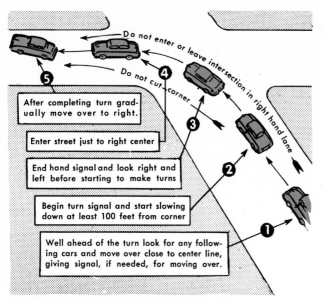

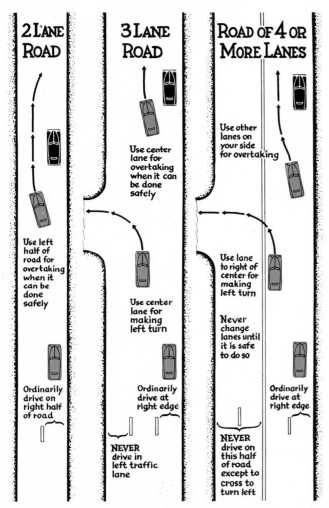

MAKING A LEFT TURN

DRIVE IN PROPER LANE

American Association of Motor Vehicle Administrators and National Safety Council.

MAKING A RIGHT TURN

and has indicated this by the proper signal. But it is illegal to pass a car going in the same direction or turning left if you have to turn out on the shoulder to do so.

After passing another car it is a good rule not to pull in front of it until you can see the car in your rearview mirror.

5. Make Turns Correctly. If you are planning to make a right or left turn, move into the proper lane well ahead of time after you signal your turn. Turning from the wrong lane by cutting in front of other cars is dangerous and illegal. Slow down for a right-hand turn so you can make it safely and not have to pull out wide. When making a left turn, drive straight to the center of the intersection and wait for traffic in the opposite lane to pass before making your turn.

WHO HAS THE RIGHT OF WAY?

The question of who has the right of way at an intersection is a frequent cause of misunderstanding and argument between drivers. The principal rule to observe is that a car approaching on the cross street *on your right* has the right of way—unless, of course, you are on a through street. Likewise, a car approaching on your left should give *you* the right of way. Other rules to remember are:

1. The car that has already entered the intersection has the right of way over the car just approaching.

2. A driver waiting to make a left turn must give the right of way to cars coming from the opposite direction.

3. Drivers must give the right of way to pedestrians at intersections.

4. A driver coming out of a driveway or alley must give the right of way to passing cars in the street.

Needless to say, even if you are entitled to the right of way, it is better to yield it to the other driver rather than risk a collision. Legally, the driver who has the "last clear chance" to avoid an accident is responsible if he does not do so, regardless of who has the right of way. Remember Jonathan Gray:

> Here lies the body of Jonathan Gray
> Who died while taking the right of way.
> He was right, dead right, as he sped along,
> But he's just as dead as if he'd been wrong.

In bringing your car to a stop at an intersection, even though there are no pedestrian crosswalk lines, stop so the car does not block the pedestrian crossing area. No pedestrian should have to turn from his path to walk around the front or rear of your car when crossing the street.

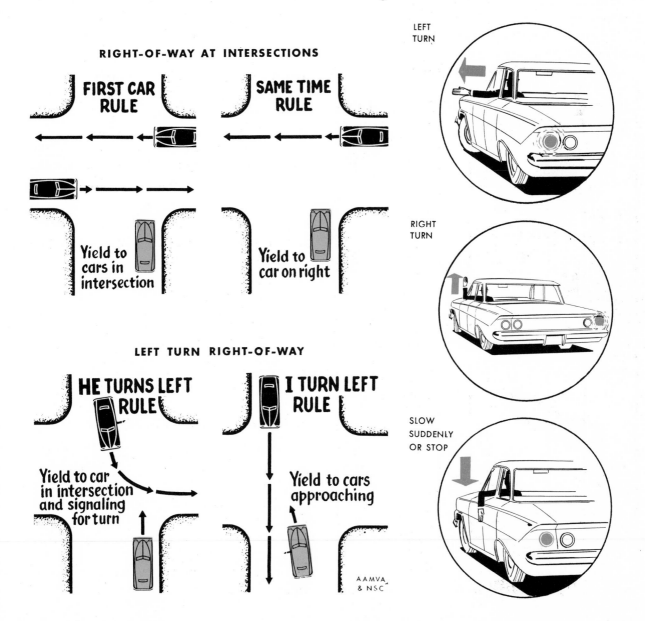

PARALLEL PARKING

It is important to be able to park your car quickly and efficiently so that on a busy street you will not obstruct other drivers more than necessary. As you slow down and prepare to park, signal with your directional lights.

Be sure the space you select is large enough to take your car. Check all traffic, then pull up parallel with the car ahead and stop. Now turn your steering wheel to the right and ease your car backward into the parking space. When your front seat—or some other part of your car you have determined by previous practice—is in line with the rear tail light of the parked car, start turning your steering wheel to the left as you continue to back slowly. This will straighten out the rear end of your car so that you will not run over the curb. Continue to back, watching carefully so that you do not ram into the car parked behind. When you are alongside the curb, turn your steering wheel to the right again to straighten out your front wheels, and then pull ahead enough to position your car evenly between the two cars.

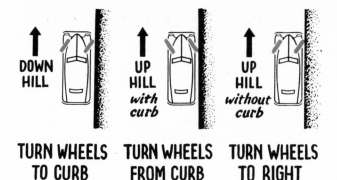

TURN WHEELS TO CURB   TURN WHEELS FROM CURB   TURN WHEELS TO RIGHT

AAMVA and NSC

PARKING ON A HILL

When you have to park heading downhill, turn your front wheels so that they are at a sharp angle heading into the curb. When heading uphill on a street with a curb, turn your front wheels sharply away from the curb. If there is no curb, turn your wheels sharply toward the road edge. In cars with manual gearshifts, place the shift lever in reverse when headed downhill and in first gear when headed uphill. In cars with automatic transmission, the "parking" indicator will lock the wheels. But as an added precaution, set your parking brake when parking on a slope.

PARKING PRECAUTIONS

When entering or leaving a parked car, it is safest to use the door next to the curb. But if this is impossible for some reason, and you enter or leave on the left side, be certain no car is approaching before you open the door. Likewise, when preparing to pull out of a parking space, wait for a break in the traffic and look carefully for oncoming cars before moving away from the curb. Always signal before you pull out. The careless or reckless driver who zooms out into a lane of traffic without looking is a menace. So is the one who opens his door on the left suddenly to leave the car.

Parking regulations are for your safety and convenience. Observe them to the letter. Watch for fire hydrants and do not park closer than the law provides. Park close to the curb and within the painted markings, if there are any. It is safe to say that double-parking is illegal everywhere.

PARKING BETWEEN CARS

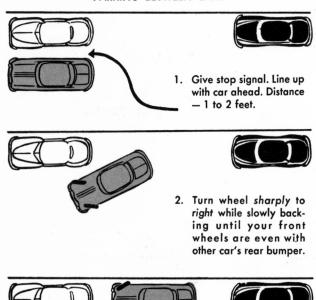

1. Give stop signal. Line up with car ahead. Distance — 1 to 2 feet.

2. Turn wheel *sharply* to right while slowly backing until your front wheels are even with other car's rear bumper.

3. Turn wheel *gradually left* until your front bumper clears car ahead. Pause, then turn wheel *rapidly* full left while slowly backing into place. Go slowly forward, straightening wheels slightly.

The Greyhound Corporation

JAYWALKERS AND OTHER HAZARDS

Pedestrians. One of the most serious hazards of city driving is the pedestrian who tries to cross streets "against the lights," or who steps from between parked cars into the path of oncoming traffic. Even worse is the hazard of the child who darts into the street from between parked cars. So in driving along a street lined with parked cars, train yourself to watch for any indication of either adults or children starting to cross in front of you.

Children. When you see children playing on the sidewalk or anywhere near the street, slow down and be especially careful. Children, even older boys and girls, act on the spur of the moment and are apt to dart out into the street without warning, especially if being chased or trying to recover a ball. Be watchful when driving through residential areas, near schools or playgrounds, or any place where children congregate.

Cyclists. Always give a wide berth to children or adults on bicycles. If traffic permits, swing toward the center of the street, or even into the opposite lane while passing. Cyclists should, of course, keep to the curb lane, but you never know when one may lose his balance or make an unexpected turn. Don't try to blast them out of the way with your horn. A light warning toot may be necessary as a signal you are coming past, but never do anything that might panic a rider.

Taxis and Buses. Be on the alert for taxicabs which may swerve into the curb to pick up passengers. Look out for streetcars and buses where passengers may leave by a rear door or pass around in front to cross the street. It is a good practice to stop behind a standing trolley or bus. In most states no driver may pass a school bus either way while children are alighting from or boarding it. Check state and local regulations to be sure. Police cars, ambulances, and fire apparatus always have the right of way. When you hear a fire or police siren, pull over to the curb if possible, or stop where you are until the vehicle has passed.

HAZARDS OF CITY DRIVING

Absent-minded pedestrians.

Children and buses.

Cyclists in traffic.

Fire, police, or hospital vehicles.

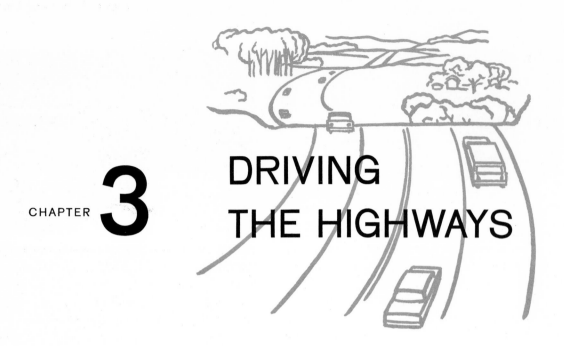

CHAPTER 3 DRIVING THE HIGHWAYS

ON COUNTRY roads and highways your ability as a good driver is further tested. Although traffic is less, the higher speeds and the variety of driving conditions you may encounter make attentive driving especially important.

HIGHWAY PASSING

As you know, passing another car on a highway is somewhat different from passing in city traffic, since both cars will be going at higher speeds. Consider this: In passing a car going 35 miles per hour you must travel the distance of 18 car lengths—that is, about 360 feet—before you are in front of it. Passing a string of trucks requires even greater caution. Usually truck drivers leave about 150 feet clearance between trucks so that a passing car can cut back in when necessary.

When you are planning to pass a car ahead of you, steer a little toward the center of the road so that you will have a better view ahead, check your rearview mirror, then signal your intention to pass with your directional signals, horn, or with a flash of your headlights. Make it an absolute rule never to overtake another car at an intersection, or in any situation where you are not certain you can pass easily and without danger to others, and yourself. If you have the slightest doubt—don't!

Give yourself plenty of room when passing another car. If you "brush by," a slight swerve by the other driver might cause a serious accident. Always be on the lookout for the car behind, too. The driver of that car may be thinking of passing you, but he'll change his mind when you give him the proper signal.

It is positively against the law—as well as foolhardy—to follow a car closely when it is passing another car. Of course, if you could know exactly what the other fellow is going to do you might get by with it. But how can you know he is not going to cut in sharply ahead of the car he is passing, leaving you no room to follow? You would then be forced into the lane of oncoming traffic and would have to put on enough speed to pass the car you were following to get ahead to safety.

OOPS! YOU'RE OFF THE ROAD

If you are forced to leave the pavement because of oncoming cars or other hazards—or because of your own careless driving—do not under any circumstances try to swerve your car back onto the road.

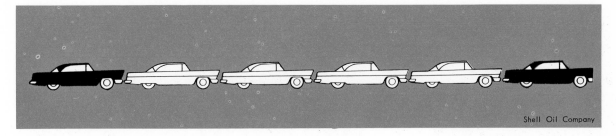

Shell Oil Company

For each 10 miles of speed, allow at least one car length between your car and the car ahead. At 40 m.p.h., stay 4 lengths behind; at 50 m.p.h., stay 5 lengths behind, etc.

Grip the wheel firmly and keep your wheels straight. Do not brake until the car is straight on the shoulder. Then pump your brakes until you are slowed down to well under 20 miles per hour. When the shoulder is too soft for braking, allow engine compression to slow the car by removing your feet from the brake and clutch pedals. Do not try to get back onto the road until the car is slowed down and completely under control.

It is hoped you will never meet an oncoming vehicle heading toward you on the wrong side of the road at a speed of 40 miles per hour or more. But if you do, and there is no way to avoid a collision, it is better to leave the road and take your chances. Yielding objects such as fences and bushes will help to check your speed. Brake strongly. The first second of braking will kill off more energy than the second or third.

MAKING A U-TURN

There may be times when you will want to make a U-turn on a busy two-lane highway.

If traffic is heavy and fast from both directions, pull out onto the right shoulder and stop at an angle which will give you a good view both ways. When there is a break in the traffic, pull across the pavement in low gear, complete your turn on the opposite shoulder, shift to second gear to regain speed, and then get back onto the pavement at the first opening. If your wheels begin to spin as they approach the pavement, reduce power so the spinning stops before the wheels reach the pavement.

U-turns are illegal in some states. You will then have to drive until you find a lane or driveway that will give you room to turn. Prepare to stop, signaling with your lights and horn; then back into the lane and wait until the road is clear and you can pull out into direction you wish to go.

When stopping or parking your car you should, of course, be completely off the road.

ON HILLS AND CURVES

You can never know what may be just over the crest of a hill, or around a curve, even in your own lane. There may be a stalled car, a fallen tree, or a wandering animal. So go slowly. Remember this rule of the road on hills:

A driver coming down a hill should always

PASSING DISTANCE REQUIRED						
Your Speed (m.p.h.)	20	30	40	50	60	70
No oncoming traffic						
Your speed 10 m.p.h. greater than car you are passing, you need	240 ft.	480 ft.	800 ft.	1200 ft.	1680 ft.	2240 ft.
Your speed 15 m.p.h. greater than car you are passing, you need	160 ft.	320 ft.	533 ft.	800 ft.	1120 ft.	1493 ft.

Note: If there is oncoming traffic, you will need double the above distances for safe passing.

Mountain driving calls for skill and steady nerves.

make it easy and safe for the driver coming up. Stay well on your side of the road. If you have an accident while driving out of your lane, you are held responsible.

Coasting down a long slope in neutral—with the clutch disengaged—is unsafe and illegal. For one thing, it places an unnecessary strain on the brakes and they might "fade out" on you. Keeping the car in gear provides a braking action.

A good practice is to go down a hill in the same gear you would use going up. This may mean shifting into a lower gear—down-shifting or double-clutching—when you are using a manual gearshift. This is how to do it: (1) Lift your foot from the accelerator and at the same time push clutch pedal to the floor. (2) Move the gear stick into neutral. (3) With stick in neutral, let out clutch and give accelerator a quick, light jab. (This co-ordinates gear speed with engine speed.) (4) Push in clutch and immediately shift from neutral to next lower gear. (5) Let out clutch the instant the gear stick falls into the lower gear. All this in a matter of seconds. Practice!

Parking on a hill may sometimes be necessary. Observe the same rules as given in city parking for such conditions. If you have to stop in traffic on a hill, engage the hand-brake to keep the car from rolling.

If you want to start down or back up on a hill from a parked position, keep the hand brake engaged. Start the engine and put the car in first gear or reverse, as the case may be. Accelerate and release the hand brake, at the same time gradually engaging the clutch.

MOUNTAIN DRIVING

In thin mountain air, your motor will heat up more rapidly, especially on a warm day. If your engine becomes overheated after a long climb, stop the car but do not turn off the engine immediately. Let it idle for a short time to keep the water in the radiator from boiling and to keep the gas from being cut off by excessive heating.

Remember that in going up you are always pulling against gravity. If your car has 100 horsepower at sea level it has only 82 horse-power at 5,000 feet, and only 60 horsepower at the top of Pikes Peak. This means that you will have less power for accelerating and passing another car, so be especially careful when passing on an upgrade. On a down-grade, guard against building up too much speed, or your car may go out of control.

Mountain driving calls for extra care in every way. Most accidents in mountain driving are caused by drivers swinging to the wrong side of the road, either because of too much speed on curves, or because of hugging the center line too closely to avoid a drop-off on the right. Avoid stopping on a mountain road unless you have room to pull off on the shoulder completely. Be wary of sudden weather changes, and watch for signs about road conditions ahead. In short, if you are not accustomed to long steep grades, curves, and drop-offs, you had better let someone else take the wheel.

CURVES—RIGHT AND LEFT

A curve to the right is more difficult to negotiate than a curve to the left because on a right curve you are on the inside lane and must turn at a more acute angle. On a curve to the left you will be on the outside lane and have a wider area to turn.

Going too fast around a right turn may throw you into the lane of traffic coming the other way. But going too fast around a left turn may throw you off the road.

Slow down when approaching a curve, but accelerate on the curve itself. This will help to overcome centrifugal force—the tendency to go outward. This is good driving.

If for some reason you have to brake on the curve itself try, if possible, to keep the front wheels straight at the instant of braking. Apply brakes in quick hard jabs and turn the wheels to follow the curve when brakes are released. Repeat. However, such a maneuver should not be attempted on a sharp curve.

DRIVING THE EXPRESSWAYS

Driving the expressways—which is the general name for thruways, parkways, turnpikes, superhighways, tollways, and all types of divided highways with planned entrances and exits and little or no cross traffic—requires special techniques and precautions. Be sure you have enough gas and that your tires are in good condition. You can be fined for running out of gas on a toll road in some states, so be careful.

Never pass on curves is one of the basic rules of safe driving. This illustration shows two types of hazards you might meet if attempting to pass on a curve.

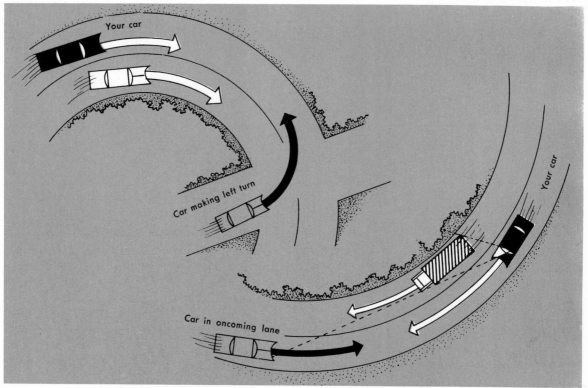

ENTERING AND LEAVING EXPRESSWAYS

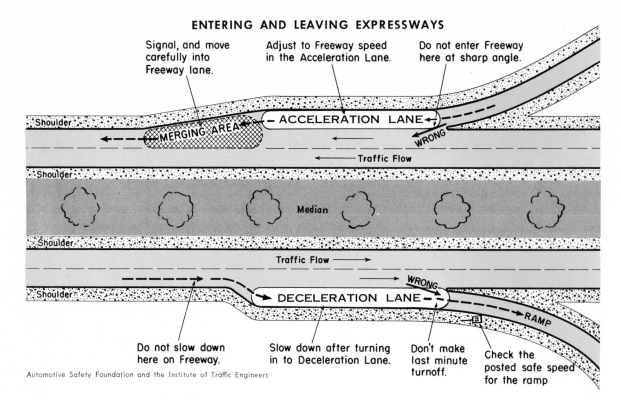

Signal, and move carefully into Freeway lane.

Adjust to Freeway speed in the Acceleration Lane.

Do not enter Freeway here at sharp angle.

Shoulder

MERGING AREA

ACCELERATION LANE

WRONG

Traffic Flow

Shoulder

Median

Shoulder

Traffic Flow

Shoulder

DECELERATION LANE

WRONG

RAMP

Do not slow down here on Freeway.

Slow down after turning in to Deceleration Lane.

Don't make last minute turnoff.

Check the posted safe speed for the ramp

Automotive Safety Foundation and the Institute of Traffic Engineers

First is the matter of getting onto the expressway. From a very slow speed, or possibly a dead stop, you must within a matter of seconds and in a distance of a few hundred feet become a part of the flow of expressway traffic moving along at a speed of from 45 to 60 or more miles per hour.

As you approach the expressway, you will probably find a strip of pavement extending a short distance along the right-hand side of the expressway and leading into it. This is known as the "acceleration lane." You utilize this lane to bring the speed of your car up to that of the traffic with which you are to merge. Use your left turn signal and check carefully for oncoming cars on your left to be sure none are approaching that might endanger your car, and that in merging you will not be interfering with the smooth flow of traffic.

On many expressways it is just as illegal to fall under the minimum speed limit as it is to exceed the maximum speed limit. You will probably be driving at a higher speed than you would use on regular highways, so you should give yourself an extra margin of safety, in all ways.

Look Ahead—and Behind. Look farther ahead and plan farther ahead. Leave a wider space between your car and the car in front. Beware of impulsive actions. If you plan to pass another car, for instance, check carefully to see that the left lane is clear behind you, use your left turn signal, and then turn out into this lane in a long arc. Turn back into the right lane only after you get a full view of the car you have passed in your rearview mirror. Use your right turn signal before turning.

Check your rearview mirror often when you are on the expressways. It is usually the car coming up behind you at high speed that causes damage in a crash.

Watch Traffic Signs. Pay close attention to signs on the expressways, especially the overhead signs. They are there to be read and obeyed. Speed limits vary and when such signs give their warning, obey promptly.

Watch for signs that will inform you how far it is to the next gas station, or the refreshment area, or your exit. When you decide to pull into a refreshment or rest area, or to leave the expressway, make your plans long ahead and be certain conditions are right. Always signal your intentions.

Keep to the Right. On a one-way, multilane expressway, the left lane or lanes are usually for passing only. There is no such thing as a U-turn, and where the signs read DO NOT CROSS MEDIAN, *do not cross.* You must not stop your car on the expressway, not even on the shoulder, except for an emergency.

On some expressways there are markers placed at every mile. As you drive along, check your speedometer by observing just how long it takes to go from one marker to the next. For example, if you are driving at 60 miles per hour, it should take you just one minute to cover the distance between markers.

You can check your odometer, too. The odometer registers the number of miles traveled and should click off a mile each time you pass a mile marker. Keeping your mind occupied thus will break some of the monotony of steady driving, and by changing the focus of your eyes you will relieve them of continually looking straight ahead.

Despite the speed allowed on expressways, there are fewer accidents than in heavy city traffic. But when such accidents do occur they are more serious and usually result in more fatalities.

Leaving the Expressway. Three things should be remembered in leaving the expressway. First, give the proper signal. Second, follow the directional signs. Even if the sign indicates that you should turn north when you want to go south—turn north! With the intricate entrances and exits of cloverleaf intersections, you will find in the end that the sign is correct.

The third thing to remember is that once off the expressway you must readjust your driving. After turning off into the deceleration lane to leave the expressway, you suddenly find yourself in a slower speed zone, with traffic lights and stop signs, unposted intersections—and pedestrians.

TIPS FROM THE PROS

1. Train yourself to watch the left front wheels of oncoming cars for signs of swerving in order to avoid surprise turns.

2. Watch not only the car directly in front of you, but the car ahead of it, for signs of slowing. This will allow you more time to slow down or stop your own car.

3. Watch cars parked at the side of the road. A sudden spurt of smoke from an exhaust pipe may mean the car is about to pull out into traffic.

4. Always come to a complete stop at intersections where a stop is required. Training yourself to do this will make quick emergency stops more automatic.

5. Always signal all moves early and correctly with your directional signals or by hand. "Too little and too late" signals are little better than none.

6. Lock all doors from the inside. In case of a collision, this will keep you from being thrown out of the car.

7. When parking on the shoulder is necessary, day or night, leave your parking lights on and the right turn signal flashing.

8. Learn to accelerate and to brake evenly and smoothly. An expert driver is a *smooth* driver.

SPECIAL DRIVING PROBLEMS

CHAPTER 4

UNUSUAL weather or road conditions create problems even for the most experienced driver. Night driving requires special alertness and keen vision; it is far more difficult to recognize objects or to judge distances at night than in daylight. Rain or fog add other complications and may make driving hazardous by cutting down visibility. Driving on ice and snow requires special techniques to avoid skidding or getting helplessly stuck in ruts. One of the marks of a really expert driver is his skill in handling his car in such situations.

NIGHT DRIVING

Accidents on the roads and highways almost triple after dark, and almost twice as many occur in rural areas as in cities. The better lighting and lower speed limits in urban districts help to hold down the accident rate in those areas, but out on the highways the temptation to drive at high speeds may lead to tragic results. Early dusk, especially in winter when the light is so deceptive, is the most dangerous period of the day.

Don't overdrive your lights. Remember that even with the strongest headlights the distance you can see ahead is fairly limited. Dirty or dim headlights or a dirty or wet windshield reduce visibility even more. Keep your speed down to the point where you *know* you can stop safely if some object suddenly looms up ahead; don't rely on swerving or dodging, or you may find yourself off the road and in the ditch. Cars parked on the edge of the road without lights, and wandering animals, are frequent hazards.

The momentary blindness caused by the glare from the headlights of an approaching car is another hazard of night driving. Your eyes, accustomed to comparative darkness, require from seven to ten seconds—440 feet at 40 miles per hour—to adapt to the change of light, and after the car has passed, there is another period of readjustment. During such periods a pedestrian in dark clothing, or a parked car, is almost invisible.

Lower Those Lights! Both as a courtesy and as a safety measure, always switch to your low-beam headlights well in advance when meeting another car, as well as when following, and trust that the other driver will do the same. But even if he doesn't, your action may help avoid a collision. Avoid looking at the lights of the approaching car, and do not try to steer your course by the center line in the pavement. Instead, hug the right-hand side of the road, look straight ahead, and take no chance of the other car swerving over the center line.

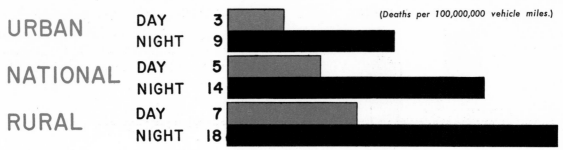

			(Deaths per 100,000,000 vehicle miles.)
URBAN	DAY	3	
	NIGHT	9	
NATIONAL	DAY	5	
	NIGHT	14	
RURAL	DAY	7	
	NIGHT	18	

National Safety Council

Motor vehicle accidents almost triple after dark.

FOG AND RAIN

Fog and rain, by reducing visibility, also reduce your ability to judge stopping distances. Your lights will not penetrate fog and rain at night. The lights reflect on the drops of water, forming a white wall which conceals warning signs and possible dangers on the road ahead.

Cut down your speed under such conditions and drive cautiously, keeping well over on your side of the road. Keep your windshield wipers going and use your defroster if necessary to prevent accumulation of frost or condensation on your windshield. Keep the rear window clean, too. Use your lower-beam lights to lessen the reflection. So-called "fog-lights" are no more effective than regular headlights properly adjusted. If you stop, tap your brake pedal to make your stoplights blink. Rear-end collisions are a special hazard in a fog. In heavy downpours, or when fog is thick or extensive, pull off the road altogether and wait for conditions to improve.

HAZARDOUS ROAD CONDITIONS

When driving on wet or icy pavements, or in mud or soft snow or loose sand, the first thing to do is to get the "feel" of the road. Keep your speed to an easy pace until you feel sure you can cope with such conditions.

Remember that when it first rains the dust and dirt on the pavement turn to mud. The road is more dangerous at the beginning of a rain than later when the surface has been washed clean. Also, any residue of grease or oil on the road will form an oil slick that is hazardous. You can usually spot this.

When driving on icy pavements, accelerate slowly and avoid sudden stops or quick turns. Watch the traffic and the lights ahead and allow yourself plenty of time to stop when necessary. Pumping the brakes will help to bring the car to a gradual stop without risk of swerving or skidding. Remember that it takes much longer to bring your car to a stop on a slippery pavement than on a dry pavement, and the greater your speed, the greater the

Allow for reduced visibility when driving in fog.

On icy pavements, reduce speed, brake slowly.

GETTING OUT OF A SKID

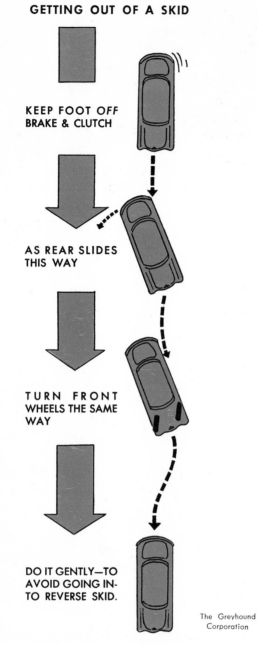

KEEP FOOT *OFF* BRAKE & CLUTCH

AS REAR SLIDES THIS WAY

TURN FRONT WHEELS THE SAME WAY

DO IT GENTLY—TO AVOID GOING IN- TO REVERSE SKID.

The Greyhound Corporation

You can rock yourself out of a rut.

braking distance required. Snow tires, with their deep treads, are useful on snow-covered streets, but experiments show that tire-chains are the most efficient means of reducing braking distances on ice.

WATCH THAT SKID!

Skidding can occur on any kind of wet or slippery surface and is usually the result of carelessness—a little too much speed, an abrupt turn or swerve, failure to observe the condition of the pavement, or sudden braking or acceleration.

A skid usually takes you by surprise and your first impulse is to jam on the brakes. This is the wrong move, as it simply makes the skid worse. Instead, turn your front wheels in the direction the rear of the car is skidding, and pump the brakes cautiously. Be ready to turn the wheel in the opposite direction to help the car straighten out. As it begins to straighten out, straighten your front wheels also. This should correct the skid, and you can then proceed at reduced speed.

Watch out for shady spots on the road where ice may form even after the rest of the road is clear, and be careful of slippery surfaces on roads going over bridges or viaducts. Be careful, too, of areas covered with wet leaves—these can be as slippery as mud or ice.

WHEN YOU GET STUCK

Getting your car started from a dead stop on a slippery surface such as snow or ice, or in deep sand or a muddy rut, is often a problem.

Don't become impatient and try to rush the car. Take it easy. First, be certain your front wheels are straight. If they are turned, the rear wheels will not receive equal power; one will idle, as if going around a curve.

If the surface is merely slippery, it is best to start off in second or high gear. Use little power, so that your wheels will not spin.

If you are stuck in snow, mud, or sand, the best method is to "rock" your way out. Start forward easily in low gear and then quickly change to reverse. Don't force the car or spin your wheels, or you will just deepen the rut.

Shift back to low again, and again reverse. As the rocking backward and forward increases you gain a little more each time, and suddenly you are clear. In bad driving weather it is wise to carry a small bag of sand in your car which you can use to spread under the wheels and help them gain traction.

COLD WEATHER DRIVING

Getting your car started—and keeping it going—is the constant problem of winter driving, especially during extremely cold weather. Experts now advise that you should not race your motor or let it idle to "warm it up." The best way to warm it up is to get the car under way as soon as you can without stalling the motor, and run at moderate speeds so that the oil and coolant will circulate. Remember that cold weather cuts down the efficiency of your battery and it will therefore need checking and perhaps re-charging more frequently than in mild weather. A battery operates at its maximum efficiency at 80° F., and efficiency decreases as the temperature goes down.

Don't let snow accumulate on top of your car or build up under the aprons. The added weight can make quite a difference in your car's gas consumption.

Also, keep the gas tank at least half full all the time. This will help prevent vapor from forming water in the gas line and freezing—another cold-weather hazard that can be very troublesome. However, most gasolines now have a gas-line antifreeze additive.

BRAKING DISTANCES ON VARIOUS SURFACES AT 20 MPH

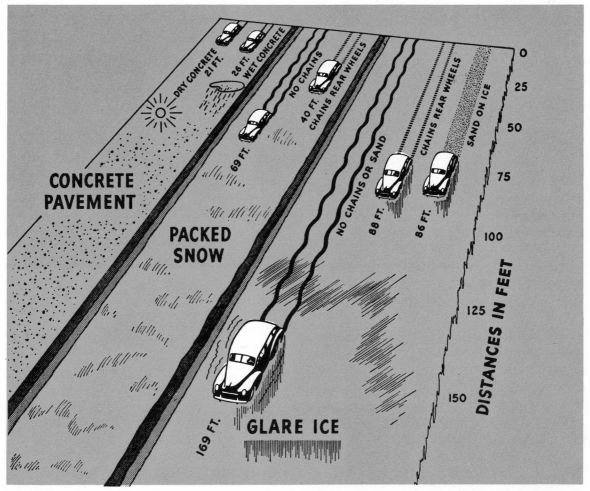

AAMVA and NSC.

CHAPTER **5** COLLISIONS ARE NOT ACCIDENTS

IF YOU have a collision or are involved in a collision it is for one of two major reasons: 1. Your failure or the other fellow's failure to adjust to conditions—driving too fast, ignoring traffic rules, etc. 2. The mechanical condition of your car or the other car, such as outright brake failure.

This is why traffic experts insist that collisions do not occur accidentally but are caused.

HASTE MAKES—COLLISIONS

The Number One cause of collisions is not speed but HASTE. Controlled speed is essential to today's driving, but hurry, impulsiveness, scramble, competitiveness, or reckless, wasteful speed have no place in safe driving practices.

Bad weather, such as icy or wet pavements, fog or heavy rain, is often listed as the "cause" of a collision. But bad weather is only an adverse condition to which the driver must adjust himself and his driving. The worse the weather the more cautious you must be— even to the point of stopping until things get better.

Bad roads play only a small part in collision cases—a mere 5 per cent. Ruts, bumps, or loose gravel, for instance, are conditions which should simply make you more cautious. At least 95 per cent of traffic collisions—and 80 per cent of fatal collisions—occur while drivers are proceeding straight ahead in clear weather with highway conditions normal.

The real causes of collisions in such conditions are usually driver faults—failure to watch traffic lights, failure to use the proper turn signals, failure to yield the right of way, improper turning maneuvers, and the all-around lack of good driving principles or sportsmanship.

The rear-end collision is the most common type. This is usually the result of the car behind following too closely—"tailgating"— or of the car in front making a sudden, unsignaled maneuver, such as an abrupt left turn. And more collisions of all types occur on weekends and holidays.

WHIPPERSNAPPERS AND FUDDY-DUDDIES

The older driver usually blames the young "whippersnapper" for driving too fast or too carelessly. The young driver blames the old "fuddy-duddies" for stubbornness, slowness, and disregard of traffic signals. Both are right in some instances. Men blame women for causing collisions, but it has been shown that

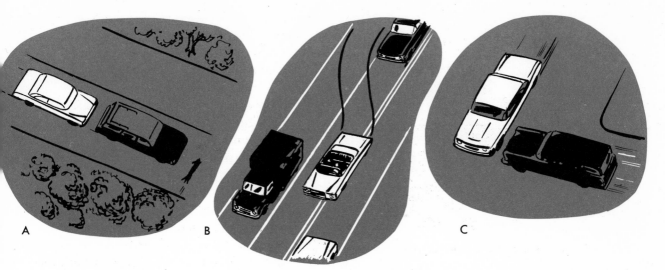

Three common causes of collisions: (A) *tailgating;* (B) *weaving in and out of traffic;*
(C) *ignoring right-of-way regulations.*

women driving competitively with men under the same conditions surpass men in avoiding collisions.

Drunkenness, of course, is the cause of many collisions, and the drunken driver is one of the worst driving hazards because his actions are so unpredictable. "Act of God" is a term often misapplied to conditions such as slippery roads, dense fogs, heavy rain or snow, and wayward dogs. The term, however, should only be used to mean natural phenomena over which the driver has no reasonable control—such as earthquakes, tidal waves, lightning, or landslides. This is the true definition of the term "accident."

WHAT TO DO IN CASE OF COLLISIONS

A collision may result in no more than a dented fender, or it may result in bodily injury or even loss of life. If you are involved in a collision—especially if another car is involved—try your best not to become excited or confused. Follow these rules:

1. Place flags or flares around the scene of the accident far enough away to enable other drivers to stop.

2. See that the injured receive emergency first aid and medical attention. Get help from the local or state police, an ambulance if needed. Do not attempt to move injured persons without skilled help, unless absolutely necessary. Cover them to prevent shock, apply bandages or pressure to stop the flow of blood, and get a doctor or someone trained in first aid as quickly as possible. Every driver should take the basic Red Cross course in first aid.

3. Obtain the name, address, and license data of the other driver and his vehicle; also

IF YOU HAVE A COLLISION

1. Set flares to warn other drivers.

2. Take care of the injured.

3. Get the names of witnesses.

4. Report to state or local authorities.

the name of his insurance company.

4. Obtain the names and addresses of as many witnesses as possible.

5. Make no statement to anyone except an officer of the law. Do not argue!

6. Above all, do not admit personal responsibility or attempt to negotiate settlement of damage claims on the scene.

7. Notify your insurance company as soon as possible.

8. Report the collision to the state authorities. In some locations the local police must be notified, and sometimes cars may not even be moved until the police arrive.

9. Draw a diagram of the place where the accident occured, showing the direction of streets or roads and position of cars.

10. Obtain the who-what-when-where-how information: Who was in the collision, what happened, when it happened, where it happened, and how it happened.

SAFETY FIRST—AND ALWAYS

No one wants to be involved in a collision, and here are a few tips on how to avoid them:

1. Adust Your Seat Comfortably. If the seat is too close to the pedals your brake reaction time will be increased because you are in a cramped position. Too great a distance from the pedals is also a handicap. Adjust your rearview mirror, too, for clear vision.

Your back should be firmly against the back of the seat. Your hands should be upon the wheel in the "ten to four o'clock" position. The ball of the right foot should be centered on the gas pedal with the left foot on the floor behind the clutch pedal. In automatic driving the left foot has nothing to do.

2. Use Your Seat Belts. Seat belts will not prevent death or injury in all types of highway accidents but they do help to prevent many injuries and reduce the severity of others by restraining the forward motion of the body in case of collision. The use of seat belts is recommended by all safety experts. They should be fastened at all times.

3. Watch Your Brakes. In damp or rainy

Keep your seat belts fastened. In case of a sudden stop or shock they will reduce the chance of serious injury.

weather brakes are apt to grab too soon. Apply gentle pressure to the brakes as you move along for 50 to 100 yards. The heat generated by the friction will dry out the moisture. Follow this practice, too, immediately after driving through any water deep enough to get the brakes wet.

4. Brake Carefully. On a slippery surface, or when traveling at high speed, stop your car by "pumping" the brake pedal rapidly, rather than by applying a steady pressure. Slamming on the brakes suddenly may result in throwing your car into a spin or skid.

SUDDEN EMERGENCIES

If Your Brakes Fail. Don't panic. Pump the brake pedal up and down quickly. If the brakes still do not catch, pull on your parking brake. Ease into lower gear as soon as possible and pull off the road.

If You Have a Blow-Out. When a tire blows out, your first impulse is to press your foot hard on the brake, but this is the worst thing you can do, as it may throw you into a skid. Hold the steering wheel firmly and keep your front wheels straight. Ease up slowly on the accelerator. When you have slowed to a safe speed, press lightly on your brakes and stop.

If Your Car Catches Fire. Pull off the road as quickly as possible. Switch off the ignition. If you have passengers, get them out. Send someone to call the police or fire department. Use your fire extinguisher from *outside* the car. Should the fire approach the gas tank, run back out of danger.

"Steady does it" when you have a blowout.

In case of fire, keep cool but act fast.

CHAPTER **6** THE LAW IS THE LAW

THE smart driver obeys the law. He knows that traffic regulations are for his protection as well as for that of other drivers. He realizes that traffic laws are the outcome of exhaustive studies by traffic engineers, safety experts, and others, and are designed to make the use of highways safer and more enjoyable for everyone.

It is the duty of the traffic policeman to enforce these laws. Cooperate with him. Do not resent or fear him, or try to evade traffic regulations. By so doing you endanger yourself, your passengers, and everyone else on the road.

IGNORANCE OF THE LAW IS NO EXCUSE

Every driver should know both local and state traffic laws and regulations, especially those in regard to speed limits, parking, right and left turns, passing, pedestrian rights, and basic automobile equipment required in relation to lights, brakes, warning devices, etc. The Motor Vehicle Division of your state will supply you with a vehicle operator's manual listing these regulations.

The traffic officer who stops you expects you to be familiar with the law or regulation you have violated. The officer will want to see not only your driver's license, but possibly your certificate of title. These should be carried at all times.

THE TRAFFIC COURT

It is when you arrive in the Traffic Court, if your violation has been a major one, that you realize the seriousness of ignoring or disobeying the law. Traffic violators when found guilty are subject to a fine or possibly to imprisonment. Their licenses may be suspended or revoked.

Suspension of a driver's license is mandatory in most states when the driver is convicted of (1) manslaughter with an automobile; (2) driving while under the influence of liquor or drugs; (3) operating a car in the commission of a crime; (4) hit-and-run driving; (5) giving false statements under oath concerning ownership of a car. Three convictions within a year on "moving violations," such as going through a stop sign or stoplight, or reckless driving, may also bring suspension of the driver's license.

Illegal parking or "non-moving violations" in many cases have fixed fines of from $2.00 to $5.00 which sometimes may be paid by mail. But where violations demand your presence in court, and especially in collision cases where there has been serious property damage or injury or death, it is best to be represented by legal counsel.

A voluntary visit to a traffic court to observe the procedure and listen to some of the cases is a good education for a conscientious driver.

YOUR LICENSE TO DRIVE

In most states you must have three types of license to drive your car legally. First, the *state vehicle license plate,* issued yearly by the State Motor Vehicle Department or the Secretary of State. Second, a *local or city vehicle license,* issued by your local community and applying only to this limited area. These two licenses certify that your car has been duly registered with the state and local authorities. Third, your personal *driver's license,* which permits you to operate a car. This is also issued by the state, usually for a period of one or more years at a time, and can be revoked or suspended by the state as a penalty for traffic violations. If you move from one state to another you must secure a new driver's license, as well as new vehicle license plates for your car.

Then, of course, there is your *certificate of title,* the card you receive with your state license plates, which identifies you as the owner of the car.

THE PRIVILEGE OF DRIVING

Driving a car is a privilege to be earned, not an automatic right. You secure a driver's license by showing that you are qualified to operate a car, and you may lose it if you violate your state's driving regulations. All states now require a driver to pass a basic driving test in order to qualify for a license, and in some states these tests are so stiff that as many as 60 per cent of the applicants fail on their first attempt. Public opinion is coming more and more to recognize the importance of sound driver education. Such training now begins in the high schools in many communities. Some states issue restricted licenses limiting drivers with certain physical dis-

A serious traffic violation may cost your driver's license.

abilities to certain speeds, or to driving only during daylight hours, or requiring the use of special mirrors and other driving aids.

The age at which you can obtain a driver's license varies from state to state, but the general average is sixteen years. In several states the age has been raised to eighteen, unless you have completed a course in driver education. Temporary licenses are sometimes issued to new drivers who have not yet passed their driving tests. Be sure to check your own state's regulations on this point.

A driver's license is absolutely necessary for the legal operation of an automobile. Therefore it is important that you do not have to relinquish it through some major traffic violation and that you renew it before the expiration date.

CHAPTER 7 KNOW YOUR CAR

YOUR automobile is a marvel of mechanical precision and engineering skill. It is composed of hundreds of parts all working together to enable you to start, stop, speed up and slow down, turn corners, back up, and so on. There are ingenious interlocking systems—the power train, ignition system, fuel system, lubricating system, and steering mechanism. To get the best out of your car, you should understand how these various parts work and how to take care of them.

WHAT'S UNDER THE HOOD

Today's car was made possible by the development of the internal-combustion engine, light in weight and high in efficiency, which gets its name from the fact that it generates its own power within itself.

Look under the hood of your car and you will see an engine block containing from four to eight cylinders. When the cylinders are arranged in a straight row, the engine is called an "in-line-four" or an "in-line-six." If the two rows are set at an angle, the engine is called a "V-type." Thus with eight cylinders, we have the "V-eight."

The cylinder itself is shaped like a metal pipe, containing at the top a spark plug and two valves—an intake valve and an exhaust valve. The intake valve brings the gasoline-air mixture from the carburetor into the cylinder; the spark plug fires the mixture, causing an explosion within the cylinder, and the exhaust valve then expels the burned gases.

Inside the cylinder is a piston, close-fitting but moving up and down easily. With each explosion of the gasoline-air mixture at the top of the cylinder the piston is driven downward.

LIKE A MAN ON A BIKE

To convert this up-and-down motion of the piston into rotary action, each piston has a connecting rod which is attached to the crankshaft. The operation of the connecting rod and the crankshaft is much like the motion of a man riding a bicycle. The foot pedal is the crankshaft and the man's leg is the connecting rod. The rider's knee moves up and down as does a motor's piston, while the foot and pedal go around in a circle as does the crankshaft.

Connected to one end of the crankshaft is a heavy flywheel. Once set in motion, the flywheel will continue to revolve and thus keep the crankshaft turning between explosions in the cylinder, or between what are called "power impulses." The crankshaft in turning transfers power to the drive shaft which causes the rear wheels to revolve, thus putting the car into motion. The crankshaft and connecting rods are enclosed in a heavy metal crankcase just below the cylinder block.

THE CARBURETOR

The above is an over-simplification of the operation of the automobile engine. Actually, it is an intricate mechanism with many ingenious devices. For example, there is the carburetor, a delicate instrument operating on the principle of a throat atomizer. Gasoline from the gas tank is pumped into the carburetor, where it is mixed with air at a ratio of about 15 pounds of air to one pound of gasoline. The proportion of gasoline and air is regulated by the choke, which in many recent models is automatic.

It is this vaporized mist or cloud of gas and air, exploded by a spark of electricity jumping between the two electrodes of the spark plug, that creates the terrific pressure of from 600 to 700 pounds per square inch in the small space at the top of the cylinder to drive the piston down.

THE COOLING SYSTEM

Since the heat generated in the cylinders of an engine can reach a temperature of from 4,000 to 4,500 degrees Fahrenheit—twice the temperature needed to melt iron—it is necessary to have water jackets around the cylinders to keep them from overheating. Water from the radiator circulated by a small pump flows through these jackets constantly, passes around the cylinders and then back to the radiator, where it is cooled by outside air passing through the radiator grill. A thermostat regulates the circulation of the water so that the engine can only heat up to a certain temperature. If the thermostat should fail, or if a leak should develop in the radiator, the engine might become dangerously overheated.

The engine block contains the heart of the combustion engine. "Power impulses" created by the explosion of gasoline vapor in the cylinders are transmitted by the action of the pistons to the crankshaft, and then on to the drive shaft.

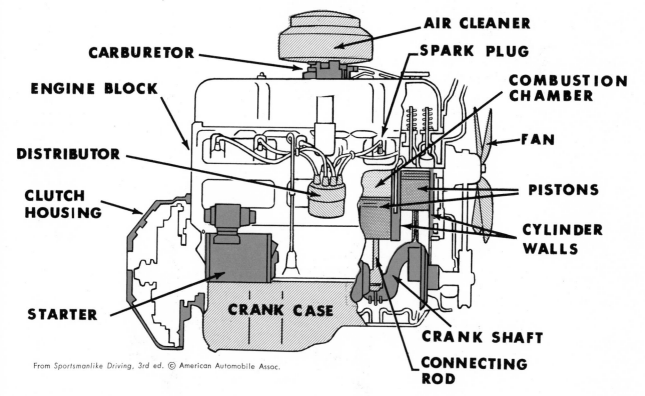

From *Sportsmanlike Driving*, 3rd ed. © American Automobile Assoc.

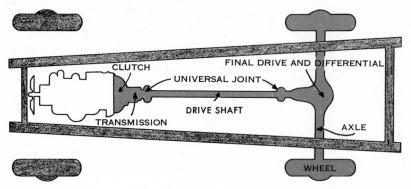

This drawing shows the main parts of the "power train," which carries the driving power created in the engine to the rear wheels.

General Motors Corp.

AUTOMATIC STARTING

In its early days, the automobile engine was started by turning a hand crank, but today the initial start is given by an electric motor. This motor runs on electricity from the storage battery, and the starter button is the electric switch. After the engine is running, it drives a generator which recharges the battery.

When you touch the starter of your car you set in motion a complicated train of events. Briefly, the ignition switch turns on the electrical system, and the battery then activates the small electric motor, which sets a flywheel to rotating. This flywheel turns the crankshaft, forcing the pistons up and down until the spark plugs ignite and start firing the gasoline mixture pumped in from the carburetor. As soon as the engine is going under its own power, the starter motor is disengaged.

THE CLUTCH

Once started, the engine can run—or "idle" —without turning the wheels. That is, it can run while the car stands still. This is possible because of the clutch, which is located directly behind the engine and in front of the transmission. When the transmission is in gear and the clutch is engaged, the rear wheels will turn. When it is disengaged, the wheels receive no power.

To visualize the clutch—in this case a disc clutch—imagine two kitchen pie tins, each mounted on its own shaft. If their faces are not touching, one can be revolved and the other will remain stationary. However, if brought together with the first tin still revolving, the second will begin to revolve or spin too, and both of the shafts attached to the tins will turn as a unit.

In a car the discs are forced together by strong springs, and are separated by pushing down on the clutch pedal. When we "step on the clutch" we are disengaging the engine from the transmission. When we "let in the clutch" by removing pressure from the clutch pedal, we are letting the power from the engine engage the rear wheels so they will turn. In cars with automatic transmission there is no clutch pedal; the engaging and disengaging action is handled automatically.

The clutch makes it possible to disconnect the engine from the power train, if desired, or to connect it when the driver wants to put the car in motion.

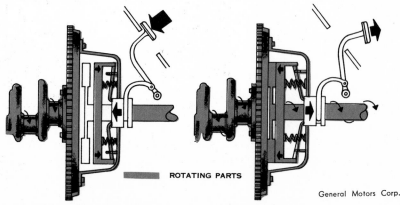

ROTATING PARTS

General Motors Corp.

Pedal Down, Clutch Disengaged   Pedal Up, Clutch Engaged

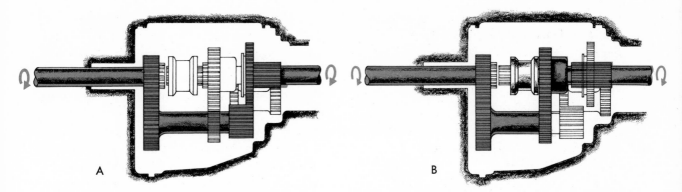

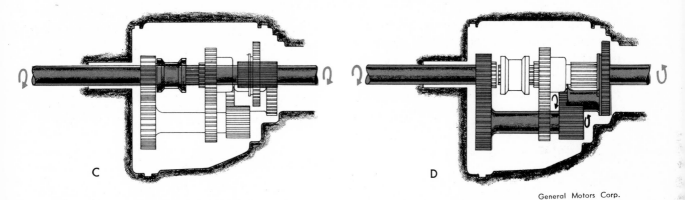

The gears of a standard three-speed transmission. (A) First gear gives power at low speed. (B) Second gear permits increased speed. (C) Third gear brings the engine shaft and drive shaft directly together. (D) Reverse uses another combination of gears to turn rear wheels in the opposite direction.

General Motors Corp.

THE TRANSMISSION SYSTEM

Proceeding now toward the rear of the car along what is termed the "drive system" or "power train" we come to the transmission system. The transmission is a combination of gears. There are small gears and large gears. When a small gear drives a large gear, speed is reduced but twisting force is increased. When a large gear drives a small gear, there is less twisting force and more speed. You can see the same principle at work in a hand-operated eggbeater where one large gear meshes with two smaller gears. Even if the large gear is turned slowly the small gears will turn rapidly, thus giving the eggbeater a high rate of speed.

First Gear. The low or first gear of an automobile is a combination by which a small gear on the engine shaft drives a larger gear on another shaft. Speed is reduced but twisting power is increased. On this second shaft is another small gear which drives a larger gear on the drive shaft which is connected

with the rear axle. This increases turning power even more. In low gear the car moves slowly but has maximum power.

Second Gear. After the wheels are turning and the car is moving, less twisting force is needed but more speed is desired. The second or intermediate gear now comes into use. In second gear the same first pair of gears is employed—the small one driving the larger one—but the second pair of gears is disengaged and a third pair engaged in its place. This pair of gears is so arranged that a larger gear drives a smaller gear, thus providing more speed.

Third Gear. When the car is well under way, a shift is made to third gear, or high. All gears are disengaged now and the engine shaft is connected directly with the drive shaft. Engine power, without the aid of the intermediate gears, turns the wheels.

Reverse. There is still another gear shift to be considered—the reverse. This is employed to back the car. The same set of gears used in first gear is used here, but a fifth gear is used between the second pair of gears. This fifth gear causes the drive shaft to twist in the opposite direction, so that the wheels turn backward instead of forward.

STICK SHIFT VS. AUTOMATIC TRANSMISSION

The shifting of the gears can be done either manually by the driver by use of a gearshift lever, or automatically by some form of automatic transmission. The manual gearshift lever, or "stick," is usually on the shaft of the steering column just below the wheel, although in some old-model cars, and some foreign makes, it emerges from the floor just to the right of the steering column.

Stick Shifting. The method of shifting with the "stick" follows the outlines of an imaginary letter H. The crossbar of the H is the neutral gear; with the stick in neutral position the car does not move. To put the car in first or low gear the stick is shifted to the lower end of the left-hand upright; to put it in second, it is shifted across neutral and into the upper end of the right-hand upright; to shift to third gear or high, it is moved down to the lower end of the right-hand upright. "Reverse" gear is the upper end of the left-hand upright. Whenever shifting from one gear to

another, the driver first steps on the clutch pedal to disengage the gears; if this is not done the gears will be badly damaged.

Automatic Shifting. In a car with automatic drive or automatic transmission the gearshift lever or stick is eliminated and there is no clutch pedal. The driver, instead, can put the car into the desired shifting position by use of a selector lever or push button. For instance, when the selector is set for "D" or "Dr," or on some cars "Dr_1" and "Dr_2" (meaning "Drive"), the gears will shift automatically as the car gains speed or slows down.

The selector lever can also be set for other positions, such as "P" for Parking, "N" for Neutral, "L" for Low, and "R" for Reverse. The selector lever is usually mounted on the steering column just beneath the wheel. In some cars it is a push-button arrangement on the instrument panel.

TYPES OF HYDRAULIC DRIVES

The Fluid Coupling. Most automatic transmissions have a hydraulic drive of some sort. One type is the "fluid coupling," which actually is a form of clutch. It resembles a doughnut which has been sliced in half, with blades inside each half. The doughnut contains oil, sealed in by a tight casing. One half is connected to the engine and the other half to the transmission.

The parts of a "fluid coupling" look like a doughnut.

The "driving member" twirls oil against the "driven member," causing it to revolve.

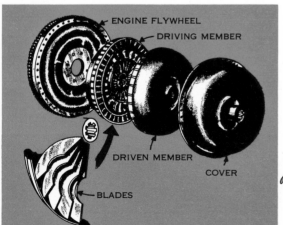

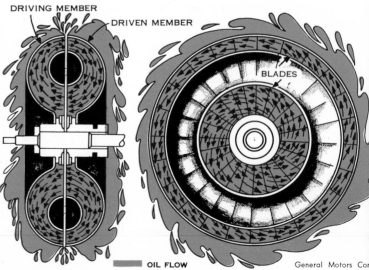

General Motors Cor

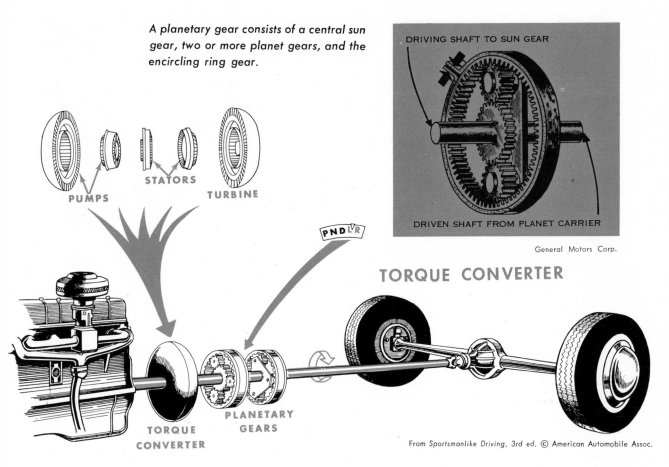

A planetary gear consists of a central sun gear, two or more planet gears, and the encircling ring gear.

PUMPS STATORS TURBINE

DRIVING SHAFT TO SUN GEAR

DRIVEN SHAFT FROM PLANET CARRIER

General Motors Corp.

TORQUE CONVERTER

PND LR

TORQUE CONVERTER

PLANETARY GEARS

From *Sportsmanlike Driving*, 3rd ed. © American Automobile Assoc.

The hydraulic torque converter works something like a fluid coupling, but also acts as a set of gears to "multiply torque."

When the half connected to the engine begins to revolve it twirls oil against the other half, and as speed increases this other half also begins to turn. At ordinary driving speeds both halves turn at almost the same speed, and when fully engaged, the coupling operates as solidly as a friction clutch.

A simple way to visualize this is to place two electric fans face to face. One fan is started and the breeze begins to turn the blades of the other fan. The fluid coupling works in much the same fashion.

Planetary Gears. In combination with the fluid coupling is a gear transmission known as the "planetary" type with gears always in mesh. Shifts are made by friction bands and clutches which grab certain parts of the transmission and hold it stationary. One such type of transmission has three planetary gearsets. One is for reverse and the other two work in

combination to provide four forward speeds. Shifting is completely automatic.

The Torque Converter. In another type of automatic transmission known as the "torque converter," the driving half and the driven half are called the "pump" and the "turbine." In addition, there is a set of stationary blades. These blades change the direction of the oil flow after it passes through the turbine, so that when it reenters the pump it helps it to pump harder. This enables it to "multiply torque"—in other words, to increase twisting force on the rear wheels, just as a gear transmission would do. Thus the hydraulic torque converter is a complete clutch and transmission in itself.

There are several variations of hydraulic torque converters, some with two sets of stationary blades and others with multiple sets of driving and driven blades.

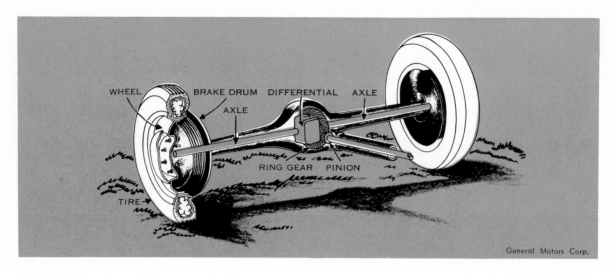

WHEEL   BRAKE DRUM   DIFFERENTIAL   AXLE

AXLE

RING GEAR   PINION

TIRE

General Motors Corp.

The "differential gear" on the rear axle makes it possible for the two wheels to turn at different speeds.

THE REAR AXLE

As we follow the drive shaft back to the rear axle we come to a mechanism known as the "universal joint." This allows the rear axle to move up and down in relation to the transmission without harm to the shaft, either by bending or by breaking. It has been likened to the gimbals of a ship compass which allow the compass to remain level regardless of the pitching or rolling of the craft.

There are two sets of gears at the rear axle. The first set is made up of a ring gear and pinion and its purpose is to transmit power at right angles to the axle shafts. A simple example of the use of the ring gear and pinion is the old-fashioned hand-operated ice-cream freezer. The pinion gear is fastened to the crank-handle shaft and the ring gear to the freezer. When the crank handle is turned, power is transmitted at right angles to the freezer, causing it to revolve. In the same way, power from the drive shaft is transmitted to the rear wheels, causing these to revolve and thus putting the car into motion.

THE DIFFERENTIAL

Next comes the "differential," a most important set of gears. The differential enables the rear wheels to turn corners properly and go around curves. When the car is making a turn, the inside wheel moves slowly while the outside wheel must revolve faster—just as when a squad of soldiers is making a turn the "pivot man" marks time while the outside men lengthen their stride. The "differential" takes care of this difference.

Two small bevel gears on the ends of the axle shaft mesh with two other bevel gears in the differential frame. The differential gear is fastened to the ring gear. All gears and the frame rotate as a unit when the car is going straight ahead and all the wheels are in line. But when making a turn, where the outer wheel must rotate faster than the inner wheel, the gears on the axle shaft—the differential—compensate for this difference. This explains why it is important to keep the front wheels straight when you are trying to start on a slippery surface. If the front wheels are turned out of line, one rear wheel will remain stationary while the other spins.

THE STEERING GEAR

It is the front wheels which determine the direction the car will take when you put it into motion, and this is true whether the motor is in the front or rear of the car.

The driver controls the front wheels by means of the steering wheel, which is mounted on the steering column in front of the driver's seat. When the steering wheel is turned to the right or to the left, this rotary motion is carried down the steering shaft to a gear box, where it is transformed into a back-and-forth motion of a rod known as the "Pitman Arm." A system of connecting rods transmits this motion to the front wheels, which respond by turning to the right or left, as the steering wheel is turned.

Many modern cars are equipped with "power steering," a hydraulic mechanism attached to the steering gear which helps the driver turn the wheel more easily.

BRAKING AND STOPPING

We have seen how power is transmitted from the engine to the rear wheels to cause the car to move. Now comes the matter of stopping the car. For this purpose brakes are provided, one for each of the four wheels.

Automobile brakes are operated on the hydraulic principle. In the brake, "shoes" covered with a special friction material are forced against the inside of a metal drum which rotates with the wheel. A system of tubes filled with "brake fluid" runs from the brake pedal to each brake, and this fluid

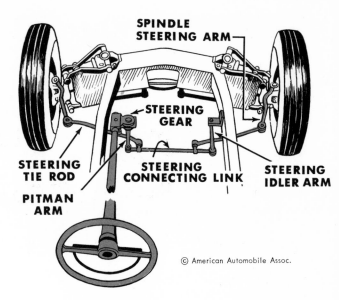

© American Automobile Assoc.

The steering wheel controls the front wheels by means of a system of connecting rods.

transmits the pressure from the driver's foot on the brake pedal to the brake shoes. A terrific amount of heat is generated by brakes in a fast stop at high speed, and so proper cooling is an important part in brake design.

Needless to say, your car needs skillful handling and care to keep all these parts operating in top condition.

Putting together the various parts discussed in this chapter, we now have the complete car.

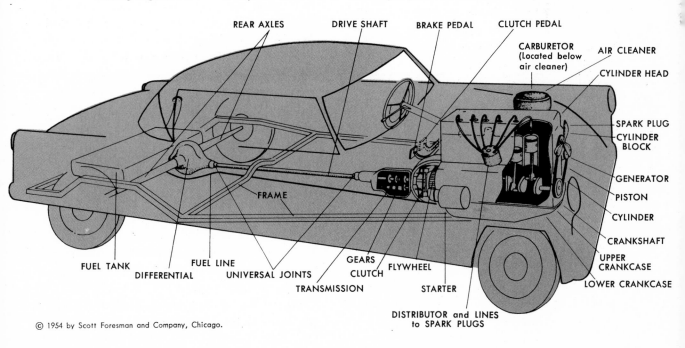

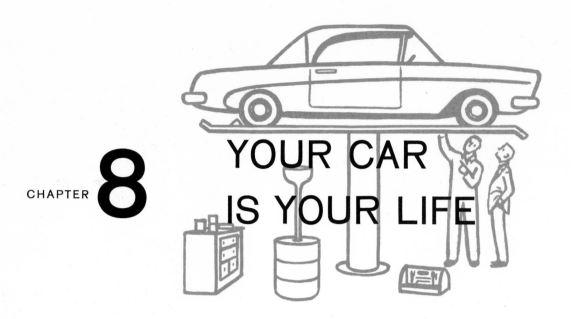

CHAPTER 8 — YOUR CAR IS YOUR LIFE

TAKE care of your car and in an emergency it will take care of you. Proper car care is not only vital to safe driving, but also to the long, useful life of the car.

See that your car has seasonal checkups. In winter it takes a terrific beating, and the best way to avoid cold-weather problems and damage is to act ahead of time. After a long hard winter, your car may expect a long hard summer. In summer, trips will be longer, with speeds and temperatures higher. So drive into your service station and have your car conditioned in the fall for winter and in the spring for summer.

SEASONAL CHECKUPS—WHAT IS DONE

Brakes (Winter and Summer). Wheels are removed and brake linings inspected. If the linings are worn, new ones will be needed. The brake fluid is checked. The parking brake is tested to be sure it will hold the car safely on a hill. If the car has power brakes, they are checked, too.

Brakes should work evenly and smoothly. If your car swerves to right or left when you apply the brakes, it is a sign the wheels are not braking evenly and need adjustment. A brake that "grabs" is dangerous in winter, for on an icy or snowy pavement it can throw your car into a skid. This is true, too, in summer on wet or muddy pavements. When pushed down hard, the brake pedal should clear the floor by at least two inches. A brake that feels "soft" and goes down to the floorboard before it holds should be corrected at once.

The Ignition System (Winter and Summer). The whole ignition system is checked, with special attention to the spark plugs, distributor points, the carburetor, the starting mechanism, lights, and horn. Dirty or worn spark plugs and points are replaced, the carburetor cleaned and adjusted, and the motor "tuned" so that it is operating at top efficiency.

Battery (Winter and Summer). The strength of the battery is tested, and if necessary it is charged to bring it up to full strength. The battery fluid is checked to see that it covers the top of the plates. Battery terminals and cables are inspected and all corrosion deposits removed and connections tightened. Wiring that has become frayed should be replaced. The voltage regulator and the generator are checked to make sure that the battery is charging normally.

During the winter the battery is called upon to work its hardest. Starting a cold motor takes a lot of current. Because of the shorter daylight hours, the lights are used for longer periods. The heater and defroster are in frequent use.

While the battery should be tested frequently both winter and summer, during the winter it needs special care. Watch your ammeter, which registers the battery charge and discharge. When proceeding at normal speeds the needle should register slightly on the charge side. (Except, of course, when the lights, radio, or heater are on.) If it does not, the ignition system should be checked.

The life of a battery usually ranges from one to three years. When your battery begins to show frequent signs of weakness and does not respond to recharging, it is probably time to get a new one. Your serviceman can advise you about this.

Radiator (Winter). The radiator is drained and flushed to remove rust and scale. Hose connections are inspected. Antifreeze is added. After this the water level in the radiator should be watched carefully. Normally there is little evaporation during cold weather. If water must be added to the radiator frequently, it is an indication that something is wrong —possibly a leak in the hose connections. If you notice a puddle under the radiator after the car has been standing over night, take your car to the service station at once.

Radiator (Summer). The radiator is again drained and flushed, and then refilled with water. It is not advisable to leave permanent antifreeze in the radiator the year round. Acid products may accumulate which could be harmful to the radiator or to the hose connections. Also, after being in use one season the antifreeze loses much of its strength. In summer a rust preventive should be added to the water.

Lubrication (Winter). Unless certain premium lubricants or oils are used which are suitable for all seasons, the crankcase, nonautomatic transmission, and differential should be drained and refilled with winter-grade oils. The winter oil should be light and thin so that it does not congeal in cold weather.

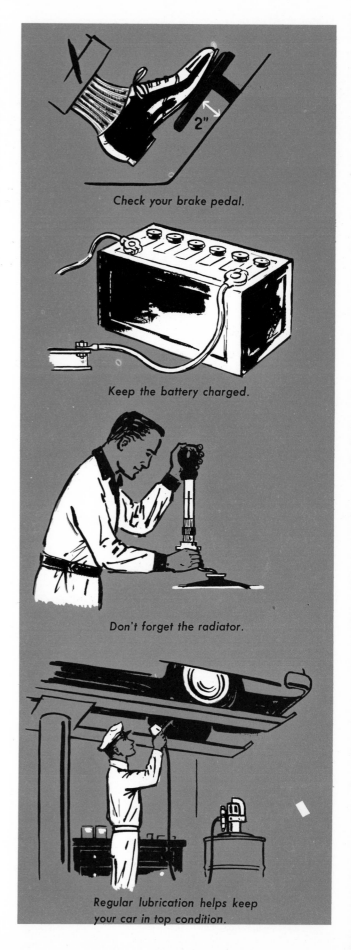

Check your brake pedal.

Keep the battery charged.

Don't forget the radiator.

Regular lubrication helps keep your car in top condition.

Lubrication (Summer). At the beginning of the summer season the winter oil is drained from the crankcase and a heavier summer-grade oil added for better engine protection during summer weather.

At the time of both the winter and summer checkups, the car should also receive a thorough grease job.

Tires (Winter and Summer). To equalize wear on the tires they should be rotated periodically, and a good time to do this is at the seasonal checkups. There are several systems of rotation and one should be selected and followed consistently. Tires should also be inspected at this time for signs of damage and aging. Tires should always be maintained at the pressure recommended by the manufacturer.

So-called snow tires are good for driving in deep, soft snow in the winter, but chains are best on hard-packed snow and on ice. There are also "winterized tires" with special gritty material embedded in the treads, which provides good traction on slippery surfaces.

Summer traveling develops high temperatures in tires, causing the air to expand. This is especially dangerous in highway travel when you may be driving at high speeds. Watch carefully for signs of wear—scuffed sidewalls, stones or nails picked up by the treads—as these may cause a blowout.

Finish (Winter). Salt and other chemicals used to melt ice and snow on streets may cause damage to the car's finish. The chrome areas, too, suffer. Whenever there is a dry spell the car should be washed. A thin coating of wax should be applied to the chrome parts. The under parts—muffler, inside of fenders, etc.—frequently are badly rusted. Many modern cars are protected by an undercoating. Those that are not should be.

Finish (Summer). This is a good time to clean the car thoroughly inside and out. A good coat of wax should be applied over the painted areas, as well as to the chrome.

Windshield Wipers (Winter and Summer). Check the arms and blades and replace with new ones if necessary.

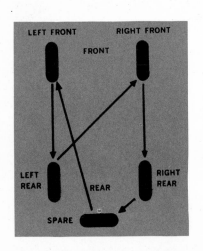

Avoid both over-inflation and under-inflation.
Rotate tires according to a regular pattern.

KEEP CHECKING AND CHECKING

Besides the winter and summer checkups, you should see that the battery and tires are checked at least every two weeks. Be certain there is sufficient water in the battery and proper air pressure in the tires. Have the oil checked frequently, and plan for a complete oil change every 1,000 or 2,000 miles (or as recommended for your particular model). This will help to keep the engine clean and running smoothly.

Each manufacturer puts out a maintenance guide for his own make of car. Following is a generalized summary of the recommended servicing at certain stages. Of course, most of this must be done by trained mechanics.

At 1,000 Miles. Drain out the break-in oil and put in the correct type of seasonal oil. Also change oil filter element. Change the rear-axle lubricant. Get a complete dealer checkup.
At Each Succeeding 1,000 Miles. Lubricate the chassis. Oil the generator. Fill the distributor hingecap oiler on all engines. Check rear-axle lubricant. Check radiator fluid level. Check brake master fluid level. Check steering gear box lubricant. Inspect tires. (Note: Some modern cars require greasing only after 30,000 miles.)
At 2,000 Miles. Change regular engine oil. Clean standard air cleaner. Clean and re-oil crankcase breather cap.
At 5,000 Miles. Have engine tune-up. Clean and refill oil bath air cleaner. Inspect spark plugs. Lubricate distributor cam and breaker pivot in a 6-cylinder engine. Check fan belt. Check brake adjustment. Rotate tires. (When rotating tires always use the spare.)

At 10,000 Miles. Repack front wheel bearings.
At 25,000 Miles. Drain and refill automatic transmission lubricant. Repack universal joints. Replace distributor cam lubricant on a V-8 motor.

"YOU'RE BURNING ME UP!"

Another good reason for careful checking of your car—apart from the safety factor—is that almost anything that can go wrong will burn up fuel needlessly. Dirty spark plugs, a defective choke or carburetor, will affect gas consumption. Worn valves and piston rings reduce motor compression and waste gasoline. Tight wheel bearings and dragging brakes prevent wheels from rolling properly, and hence your engine burns more fuel. Poor wheel alignment and under-inflated tires are also a drain on your gas tank.

HOW MANY MILES TO THE GALLON?

If you want to get the best mileage possible per gallon of gasoline, practice a few commonsense rules.

1. Start and stop smoothly. Jackrabbit starts are gas hogs. Racing your motor at a standstill eats up fuel, too.

2. Drive at a steady, moderate speed without sudden accelerations or quick stops. Of course, you get less mileage in stop-and-go driving in the city than you do in straightaway driving on the open highway.

3. Take your foot off the accelerator going down a hill and shift into low gear going up. Also, don't let the engine "idle" for prolonged periods. These minor economies mount up.

Checking Gas Consumption. To check your car's consumption of gasoline, fill your tank completely and jot down the mileage that shows on the odometer—the mileage register on the speedometer dial. The next time you get gas have the tank completely filled again, and note the mileage registered. The amount of gasoline necessary to fill the tank represents the amount used since the last filling. By subtracting the previous mileage reading from the new total, you will find out how many miles you have traveled since the last reading.

Now divide the gas consumption into the mileage and you will find how many miles you get to a gallon of gas. For instance, if you needed ten gallons of gas to refill your tank and you have traveled 180 miles since then, you are getting 18 miles per gallon.

However, this is not always an accurate measure. It is strange, but true, that many odometers will register perhaps 105 to 106 miles for every 100 miles traveled. To check this, measure your mileage on a test stretch where there are markers every mile. If this is a ten-mile stretch you may find your odometer reads 10.5 miles. Thus you can be fooled into thinking that you are getting more mileage per gallon than is actually the case.

Your speedometer, too, may show you are traveling 60 miles per hour when you are actually going only 55. Practically all speedometers register a faster speed than the car is traveling.

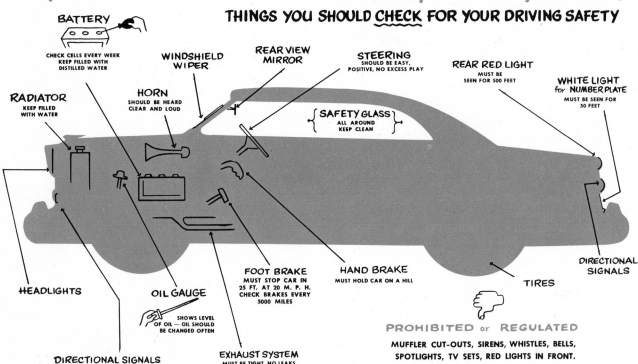

Do you know these **SAFETY CHECK** points in your car?

THINGS YOU SHOULD CHECK FOR YOUR DRIVING SAFETY

BATTERY — CHECK CELLS EVERY WEEK KEEP FILLED WITH DISTILLED WATER

WINDSHIELD WIPER

REAR VIEW MIRROR

STEERING — SHOULD BE EASY, POSITIVE, NO EXCESS PLAY

REAR RED LIGHT — MUST BE SEEN FOR 500 FEET

WHITE LIGHT for NUMBER PLATE — MUST BE SEEN FOR 50 FEET

RADIATOR — KEEP FILLED WITH WATER

HORN — SHOULD BE HEARD CLEAR AND LOUD

SAFETY GLASS — ALL AROUND KEEP CLEAN

HEADLIGHTS

OIL GAUGE — SHOWS LEVEL OF OIL — OIL SHOULD BE CHANGED OFTEN

FOOT BRAKE — MUST STOP CAR IN 25 FT. AT 20 M. P. H. CHECK BRAKES EVERY 5000 MILES

HAND BRAKE — MUST HOLD CAR ON A HILL

DIRECTIONAL SIGNALS

TIRES

DIRECTIONAL SIGNALS

EXHAUST SYSTEM — MUST BE TIGHT, NO LEAKS

PROHIBITED or REGULATED

MUFFLER CUT-OUTS, SIRENS, WHISTLES, BELLS, SPOTLIGHTS, TV SETS, RED LIGHTS IN FRONT.

FIRST AID FOR YOUR CAR

CHAPTER **9**

THE days are gone when the average car owner could afford to tinker with his car. Trained mechanics now specialize in certain makes of automobiles, and to get the best out of your car you should always have it repaired by the service department maintained by the dealer from whom you bought it, or at a service station of a dealer handling that line of car. This rule will pay off in the long run. There are, however, certain minor repairs that you should learn how to make. These are usually emergency repairs that must be taken care of on the spot—often when a service station is not available.

GET OFF THE ROAD

In case of any sudden emergency, the first thing to do is to get out of traffic and park your car so that it is in no danger from other vehicles and will not cause accidents to others. If on a city street, get your car over to the curb; if on a highway, get it completely clear of the pavement—even if this means driving on a flat tire.

On a busy thoroughfare, either during the day or night, set some signal on or near your car to indicate that it is in trouble. Your ordinary lights are not sufficient at night. A driver approaching from the rear might not realize you were standing still and would run into you. Set your turn indicator lights so they flash for a *right* turn, but also leave on your parking lights and place a red flashing light or flare 100 feet from the rear of your car.

A raised hood is a universal signal of dis-

tress among motorists, and in the event you cannot get your car started, raise the hood. The chances are a patrol car or some considerate motorist will stop and help, or will agree to send back help from the nearest service station.

HOW TO CHANGE A TIRE

A flat tire can happen to anyone at any time—so be prepared. First, pull out of the flow of traffic and set the proper signals. Then proceed as follows:

1. Set your emergency brake. Place a stone or block under the wheel diagonally opposite the tire to be changed to keep the car from rolling. If the flat is on a rear wheel, you might also turn the front wheels at an acute angle.

2. Get out the spare wheel and jack from the trunk. Before you jack up the car, remove the hubcap from the wheel with the flat end

CHANGING A TIRE

1. Get out spare wheel.   2. Pry off hubcap.   3. Loosen bolts.   4. Jack up wheel with flat tire.

5. Remove wheel and put on spare.   6. Tighten bolts and replace hubcap.

of the jack handle, or a screwdriver, prying between the edge of the rim and the wheel.

3. Next, loosen the bolts that hold the wheel in place with the socket wrench on the end of the jack handle until they can be turned by hand.

4. Place the back of the jack so that it stands straight in position with the hook under the bumper, next to the bumper guard nearest the wheel to be removed. Be certain the base of the jack is on something solid, not soft earth. Work the base down until it is resting firmly.

5. Insert the jack handle and move it up and down as you would a pump handle until the tire clears the ground and the wheel is sufficiently raised so that it can be slipped off and the spare wheel placed on. Do not raise higher than necessary.

6. Remove the loosened bolts and pull off the wheel. Place the bolts in the hubcap so they can be found readily.

7. Put on the spare wheel, and tighten the bolts by hand as much as possible. Lower the car with the jack. After the wheel is on the ground, tighten the bolts securely with the socket wrench. Place the hubcap back on and secure it with sharp blows of the heel of your hand—or a rubber hammer, if you have one.

8. Put the wheel with the flat tire in the trunk, stow the jack, and remove the stone or block from the other wheel. Have your flat tire repaired as soon as possible.

THE RUNAWAY HORN

A stuck horn is annoying, to say the least. If this should happen, give the steering column a smart thump to jar the horn. It may be that the button is jammed. If this does not work, raise the hood, and if you know the location of the horn relay switch, tap it several times. There may be a short circuit. As a last resort, unscrew the lead wire from the horn, or if it will not unscrew easily, cut the wire itself. Of course, this must be repaired by a mechanic as soon as possible.

WHEN YOU ARE LOCKED OUT

Being locked out of your car is another frustrating situation. Sometimes the lock freezes, or the key may break off in the lock, or be lost.

In the case of a frozen lock, grasp the key in a handkerchief or between gloved fingers and hold it over the flame of a match or cigarette lighter until the key becomes hot, then thrust it into the lock. You may have to repeat this several times, but eventually it should work.

When the key breaks off in the door lock and you do not have a spare key, you are in trouble. As the door key is also usually the key to the ignition, you won't be able to start the engine even if you succeed in getting into the car. It is wise to keep a spare key hidden somewhere inside the car for use in such an emergency.

You can, of course, get into the car by breaking a window, if absolutely necessary. Break one of the flipper windows, holding a stone wrapped in cloth. Wear a heavy glove and keep your head turned away to protect your eyes when you break the glass. If you cannot now reach the door-catch handle, use a strong wire, a stick with a fork at one end, or anything which you can hook onto the handle to release it.

If nothing else works, cut the wire.

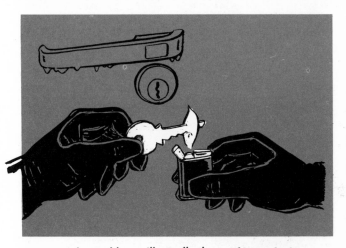

A heated key will usually thaw a frozen lock.

*Protect your hands and eyes
if you have to break a window.*

Joggling locked bumpers can be risky.

Using bricks or stones to raise the car is a safer method.

LOCKED BUMPERS

Locked bumpers are annoying and sometimes a problem. Trying to get two cars untangled can often be more dangerous than it seems. One common method is for one person to stand on the lower bumper and joggle up and down as the other car tries to pull away. Or you can try lifting the upper bumper to free the two cars. In either case, be extremely careful or you may get an arm or leg caught.

A better way is to take some bricks, blocks of wood, or flat stones—anything that will tend to raise the car—and place them under the wheels of the car whose bumper is on top. Drive the car forward or back over them. If this does not untangle the bumpers, you may have to jack up the wheels in order to raise the bumper high enough to slip free.

OTHER EMERGENCIES

Push-Starting. In case your battery is dead or so weak that the starter will not turn the engine over properly, you may have to have another car push you. If yours is a manual-shift car, depress the clutch pedal, move the gearshift lever into high, and then signal for the other car to start pushing. When your car has reached a speed of from 10 to 15 miles an hour, let out the clutch pedal, at the same time depressing the accelerator. Your engine should catch.

If you have automatic transmission, place the selector level at N (Neutral) and keep it there until your car is moving about 25 miles an hour. Now move the selector into L (Low).

Push-starting will get your car going in an emergency.

A car with manual shift may safely be towed with the front wheels elevated. But it is safer to tow a car with automatic transmission with the rear wheels elevated. Your transmission may not be working properly and you cannot be certain it is in neutral.

Vapor Lock. Vapor lock is a hot weather problem. Gasoline vaporizes in the fuel lines and the fuel pump moves this vapor into the regular fuel. In case of vapor lock, it is best to allow your engine to stand idle for a few minutes. Then, in starting, press down on the accelerator—do not pump—and hold it to the floor as you turn on the starter.

Frozen Radiator. If your radiator is frozen, the temperature indicator will register in the danger zone of HOT. Your car should be

towed or moved inside a warm garage. If this cannot be done, pour as much water as possible into your radiator and then cover your radiator grill. Start your engine and let it idle. This should thaw out the radiator.

TOOLS FOR EMERGENCIES

You should know the location of all fuses in your car—those for the lights, the horn, etc.—and how to change them. It is a good idea to carry along a box of fuses of each type used.

A Phillips-type screw driver, the kind used on four-way slotted screws, should also be added to the tool kit. Other tools useful for emergencies are:

A red flashing light, battery operated. Also a flashlight.

A carbon dioxide or dry powder fire extinguisher.

A first aid kit.

One set of tire chains, a towrope, and a ball of twine might be added.

SIGNS OF TROUBLE

Learn to watch the gauges on your instrument panel for warning signals. There are four main gauges, besides the speedometer: the oil gauge, gas gauge, battery gauge, and temperature gauge. In each, the arrow should point either straight up or to the right—except the temperature gauge, where the extreme right indicates the danger zone. By checking these gauges frequently you eliminate the danger of running out of gas, of having your

battery go dead, of your oil not circulating freely, or of the engine becoming overheated.

You can tell a lot by the color of the smoke that comes from the exhaust. Blue smoke means your car is burning excessive oil. Very dark smoke means it is consuming too much fuel. Black smoke indicates that the carburetor needs adjustment. Blue-white smoke indicates badly worn piston rings or worn valves. The best way to detect this is to have someone suddenly race a warmed-up engine while you stand to the rear and watch the exhaust pipe.

Before getting in your car after it has been standing for some time, look beneath it to see if water, gasoline, or oil has dripped on the pavement. Such dripping might indicate a leak somewhere.

TIPS ON CARING FOR YOUR CAR

1. Never press the starter when the engine is running. This may damage the starting motor.

2. In gear-shift cars, do not "ride the clutch" with your left foot. This results in needless wear and tear on the clutch.

3. Have a mechanic check the timing of the ignition system occasionally. When the timing of the spark is off, the gasoline-air mixture is not properly burned and you do not get full power.

4. Learn to slow or stop your car by "pumping" your brakes, rather than by a long, steady pressure. This keeps brakes cool and lessens wear on brake linings.

5. Study the Owner's Manual that comes with your car. This will give you specific advice on how to service your particular model, when to change the oil, what pressure to keep in the tires, etc.

6. Have the brake fluid level checked regularly—whenever the car is greased or the oil changed. Experts advise changing the fluid every six months.

LISTEN TO YOUR CAR

Listen to what your car is telling you. Many times it will complain audibly where it hurts, just as a human might groan with a stomach ache or scream when in real pain. Here are some distress calls:

Backfire. May signify improper timing of ignition or valves, a bad valve or faulty carburetor, or water in the gas.

Chatter. If in the rear, may mean warped brake drums.

Grind or Hum. Universal joint, differential, or wheel bearing trouble.

Knocks. Engine knock or clatter means the engine needs an overhaul. It might also be a fuel knock, meaning you need a better grade of gasoline. A bad spark plug will cause the engine to "miss" and run unevenly. A heavy thumping knock may mean end play in the crankshaft. Sharp, distinct knocks may mean bad bearings.

Piston Slap. A moderate metallic slapping may be caused by excessive clearance between pistons and cylinder walls, due to wear.

Rattle. May be due to faulty springs or a loose exhaust pipe.

Screech. If heard on accelerating the motor, it is usually from a loose fan belt.

Squeak. If heard when brakes are applied, it indicates worn brake linings. Brakes may also squeak when wet, but will soon dry out and return to normal. A loud prolonged shriek may indicate oil is leaking onto the brake linings.

Even if you cannot diagnose the meaning of these warning signals, it is wise to have any unusual noise checked by a competent mechanic. A car in good repair should operate smoothly and quietly; when it begins to complain, something is wrong.

SPIT AND POLISH

Take pride in your car. Keep the interior and exterior clean. Early attention to spots, scratches, and other minor blemishes will keep your car looking new and smart for a long time.

The inside of your car should be brushed each week and a real cleaning job should be done once a month. At the time of the monthly cleaning, remove the seats and use a whisk broom or vacuum cleaner to chase the dirt. Examine the upholstery for spots and stains to be removed.

Chewing gum. Use a cleaning fluid, such as benzine, to dissolve and loosen gum so it can be scraped away.

Chocolate. Use a little lukewarm water for chocolate stains, then clean with a dry cleaner.

Lipstick. Use a dry cleaner. Dampen the stain with the cleaner and blot at once.

Grease and Oil. First scrape with a blunt knife and then treat with a dry cleaner having a benzine or ether base.

Paint. Paint spots can be dissolved with turpentine, but you must work fast.

Warning

Dry cleaners or volatile cleaners should not be used on real leather. They remove the essential oils in leather and leave stains. Such cleaners, however, are safe to use on imitation leather. In case you cannot tell the difference between real and imitation leather, it is safest to use lukewarm water and a mild soap.

Do not rub nylon material too hard.

WASH—WASH—WASH—

Wash your car at least once a week. Use a sponge or cloth with cold running water. Dry with a chamois skin or cloth. If after washing you find oil or grease spots on the finish, you can take them off with a mild detergent, but wash the detergent off right away.

Dry insects can be removed with a mild solution of baking soda and water. An application of wax remover will take off tree sap.

In summer do not wash your car in the sun, as little drops of water act as burning glasses and damage the paint. Do not wash your car when the body is hot.

Washing your car in winter sometimes presents a problem, unless you have a garage. But the removal of salt and chemicals used in street snow removal is very important during the winter. In freezing weather be careful not to get water into door keyholes or around windows, as they may freeze shut.

RETOUCHING

Where paint has been chipped or rubbed off, retouch the finish to prevent rust spots from forming. You can determine the color of the body paint by looking at the paint card usually located underneath the glove compartment. Small tubes of the proper paint can be obtained from an auto accessory supply store or from the service department of the automobile agency. Buy some when you buy your car, as the shade you want may not be available after two or three years.

A protective coating of liquid or paste wax should be applied, after washing, two or three times a year. When the paint loses its luster the car should be polished. Rewax the car after polishing.

Rust may be removed from chrome with a kitchen scouring powder, and a metal paste then applied to polish the chrome.

CHAPTER 10

A CAR OF YOUR OWN

IF YOU are one of those fortunate young persons who owns a car, or is making plans to own one, you are assuming a whole new set of responsibilities and obligations. These are actually adult responsibilities, and assuming them is an extremely valuable experience.

HOT ROD OR SNAZZY CONVERTIBLE?

Some mechanically minded drivers will derive much pleasure from purchasing a Model-T Ford chassis or a broken-down heap and building it up into the car of their dreams. They know all about overhead cams, double-barreled carburetors, gear ratios, increasing cylinder capacity, and so on. And more power to them.

But the average person figures on buying rather than building a car, and as a buyer, here are some practical matters to consider.

What is your particular need for a car? Business or pleasure? What are the conditions under which you will normally drive? How many persons will be riding in your car?

Is it important for the sake of prestige to have the latest model? Or is serviceability your main concern? How much can you afford to spend in purchasing the car? What will be the costs of ownership and operation?

Having answered these questions—which should determine just what make, model, equipment, and accessories you will need— the next thing is to decide when and where to purchase the car.

WHAT ABOUT DEPRECIATION?

If you follow the want ads throughout the year you will find that the prices of both new and used cars fluctuate considerably. They go up or down according to the season and on account of varying market conditions.

Many people wait until late in the summer or early in the fall to purchase a new car and then buy the current year's model. These are usually greatly reduced just before the new models appear.

Of course, if you do buy a current model late in the year, you will have to figure that it will depreciate 30 per cent in value almost before you have it broken in. If you buy the new model for the coming year, you avoid this depreciation but pay a higher market price. Here is where you must judge carefully, taking into consideration the advantage of the reduced price with the expected depreciation, as against paying the full price on the new model.

A similar problem comes up when trading in your old car. Used car prices usually are higher in the spring, then level off in the summer, become lower when the new models appear, and are at their lowest during the winter months.

You may wish to trade in your old car after two or three years. Even though it seems in good condition and has only 20,000 to 30,000 miles on it, it is sometimes wiser to trade it in on a new car than to hold it and make repairs.

SELECT A RELIABLE DEALER

Remember, when you come to buy or trade in a car, that you are dealing with men who spend every working hour selling their product, who are familiar with the market trends, and know all the ins and outs of the business. You have perhaps picked up a few pointers here and there on how to buy a car, but there are dozens of ways an unscrupulous dealer can deceive you, and in such a fashion that the chances are you will say nothing later.

Your best protection in buying a car, as Better Business Bureaus constantly warn, is to select a reliable dealer. The honesty and dependability of the dealer is the most important factor in the purchase of an automobile. The reliable dealer is as interested in keeping your future good will as he is in protecting his own reputation. As he specializes in the make of car you buy from him, you will be assured he can supply spare parts, and has adequate servicing and repair facilities.

BEWARE OF "COME-ONS"

The Better Business Bureaus point out that some opinion of a dealer's reliability can be formed by an examination of his advertising practices. A dealer who exaggerates or misstates in his advertising is likely to exaggerate and mislead in his selling. Such statements as "Name your own terms," "We beat any deal in town," "Best deal in the city," "Wholesale prices," "We undersell," etc., are a warning to be on your guard. When such dealers boast of doing business for many years and having thousands of "satisfied customers," it is a double warning. You can bet they are smooth operators.

WHAT IS A "NEW" CAR?

New cars purchased from franchised or authorized dealers are warranted or guaranteed against defective parts or workmanship by the manufacturer. A "new car" means one that has not been registered by a private owner—thus a so-called "demonstrator," although driven many miles, can be registered as a "new" car.

However, there are many times when new cars, called "bootleg cars," are offered for sale by unauthorized dealers at what they call "discount prices." Such cars do not carry the manufacturers' warranties.

New cars must have price plainly posted.

Discuss terms fully with the salesman.

Read every word of the contract before you sign it.

THE PRICE YOU PAY

Prices on new cars are determined only in part by the manufacturers' suggested "list" prices. Actual selling prices may vary due to supply and demand, taxes, and because of the pricing policy of the dealer. These variations are often reflected in cash discounts or in the amount of trade-in allowance given. Normally, discounts and allowances are greatest during the period immediately preceding the introduction of new models.

Most dealers display prices in plain figures, and usually these prices are reasonable and not too high. Otherwise the dealer would lose customers who might be frightened away by a high price. Federal law now requires that the price be posted on all new cars.

In some cases dealers may quote a price on a new car which is several hundred dollars over that asked by competitors. This is a "cushion" to permit bargaining and enable the dealer to offer a higher trade-in allowance or a fictitious discount if no trade-in is involved. This is a form of "packing" new car prices to buyers.

"Bushing." There is another practice known as "bushing," a term applied to one of several methods of increasing the selling price of a car above that originally quoted the purchaser after the purchaser has made the initial payment, either in money or trade-in, or has signed a contract. "Open bushing" usually is accomplished by a salesman offering an exceptionally high trade-in allowance which is later repudiated by the management with the purpose of persuading the customer to turn in his car at a lower price. The original offer or order detains the customer and prevents him from looking elsewhere. "Silent" or "pencil bushing" is effected by writing in a higher selling price or a lower trade-in allowance than verbally represented, after a customer has signed an incomplete or blank contract. Never sign a contract that has not been completely filled out!

It cannot be repeated too often: *Your best bet is to buy your car from a reliable dealer,* one who is thinking of his own reputation as well as your future good will and business.

EASY WAY TO FIGURE MONTHLY PAYMENTS

Rates per $1,000 of unpaid balance in Midwestern suburban city. Finance charge is part of each payment.

Period of loan	Best terms Monthly payment	Finance charge	Good terms Monthly payment	Finance charge	Average terms Monthly payment	Finance charge	Fair terms Monthly payment	Finance charge
12 mos.	86.69	40.32	87.54	50.45	88.37	60.47	89.22	70.60
18 mos.	58.92	60.65	59.77	75.81	60.61	90.96	61.45	106.12
24 mos.	45.05	81.20	45.90	101.58	46.74	121.73	47.59	142.11
30 mos.	36.73	101.96	37.58	127.36	38.42	152.76	39.28	178.45
36 mos.	31.18	122.57	32.03	153.31	32.94	184.05	33.74	214.79

Use this chart to estimate monthly payment (which includes finance charge) on car purchased as follows:
1. Subtract down payment (including trade-in) from price of new car and equipment.
2. Divide balance by 1,000.
3. Multiply the result by appropriate figure in table.
For example, to find 36-month "best terms" monthly payment on $1,500 unpaid balance:
$1,500 ÷ 1,000 = 1.5   1.5 × 31.18 = $46.77 monthly payment   1.5 × 122.57 = $183.85 finance charge

From BUYERS' DIGEST OF NEW CAR FACTS FOR 1961. Courtesy Ford Motor Company.

The terms of your installment contract may vary considerably depending on the amount of your down payment and the length of the loan. Check carefully with a reliable finance company or bank to be sure you are getting the best terms possible.

FINANCING YOUR CAR

The best way to purchase an automobile—new or used—is to save your money and pay cash, or to pay the cash difference between the trade-in allowance on your old car and the price of the new or used car you buy. Use a budget system and lay away enough each year to buy your next car.

However, almost 60 per cent of the car buyers finance the purchase of a new car on the installment plan. If this were not so, many persons could not own automobiles. The purchaser makes a contract with the dealer to pay down in cash, or in trade, a part of the price and pay off the balance, plus or including a finance charge and usually a premium for insurance, in monthly payments.

INSTALLMENT CONTRACT

In the minds of most buyers, time-payment contracts and charges are often confused with loans and interest. The buyer speaks of the "interest" on his unpaid balance.

But this finance charge is not necessarily "interest." It is a "service charge." Nor does it necessarily mean a "loan." Although some states have laws and regulations which seek to fix finance rates or maximum charges, in most states there is no legally enforced, uniform finance charge. Thus each company determines its own "service charge."

There are different types of installment contracts in different states, but usually they are classified as *conditional sales contracts, chattel mortgage contracts,* or *bailment leases.* Rights of purchaser and seller under each type are virtually the same. Should the buyer fail to meet his payment as contracted, the car is repossessed. If after being resold the sale price does not cover the balance due with additional charges, the remainder may be collected legally from the original purchaser.

In the majority of cases the installment contract is sold by the dealer to a finance company or bank, and installment payments are made to the finance company or bank.

BUYER—BEWARE!

The Better Business Bureaus, in a "Fact" booklet series, have sought to familiarize the car-buying public with certain important points in installment purchasing.

In the first place, *never sign a contract in blank,* as is sometimes suggested by the dealer to facilitate the deal. Signing a contract in blank makes it easy for the unscrupulous dealer to "pack" the account. For example, assume that a balance of $300 is to be paid on the car. The dealer will add the finance charge and insurance premium, which may total $50. The customer agrees to pay $35 a month for ten months. *But,* had the contract been signed in blank, the unethical dealer could "pack" it by filling in a balance of perhaps $500, or $150 more for financing, insurance, etc., than in the first instance. This concealed charge is the "pack" and is rebated to the dealer or split with the finance company.

The car buyer should have his contract filled out completely, read it carefully, and then sign it and keep a copy of it. Also, he should insist on the signature of the dealer or his authorized representative, such as the sales manager—never just the salesman. Otherwise the purchase order is binding on the buyer but not on the dealer!

Money can be saved by the purchaser if the finance period can be shortened. But "balloon note" financing, a method of financing whereby the regular installments pay only a part of the debt and the final payment for the balance comes due in a lump sum, can sometimes be tricky. In many cases refinancing of the lump sum cannot be arranged, and if you haven't got the lump sum you lose the car. So be careful.

A CHECKLIST FOR BUYERS

Here is your checklist of twelve things to look for in the contract:

1. Adequate description of the car, with the name, type, motor number, and serial number, and all accessories to be included.

2. The cash price of the car.

3. The down payment on the car.

4. A description of the trade-in car, if any, and the trade-in allowance.

5. Credit allowances, if there are any.

6. The difference between the cash price and the aggregate of the down payment and allowances.

7. A description of each insurance policy for which a charge is made, and the cost.

8. The amount of the finance charges.

9. The total amount to be financed.

10. The number and amount of weekly, monthly, or other installment payments.

11. A statement of delinquency charges, if any.

12. A statement of prepayment allowances —deductions in total finance charges for paying the balance before it is due—if any, and if not regulated by law.

BUYING A USED CAR

CHAPTER **11**

EXTREME *caution should be used in purchasing a used car. Sometimes you can obtain a good, serviceable car from a used-car dealer. Or you might be able to get one from an individual, but in the latter case you will get no warranty or guarantee. Reputable new-car dealers take used cars in trade, and perhaps your best chance of obtaining a good used car, or at least one that is not misrepresented, is to buy it from such a dealer.*

KINDS OF USED CARS

Used cars are classified under two groups. First there are cars that have been "reconditioned" to put them in good working order so they can be offered for sale with a reasonable guarantee as to their condition. Such a guarantee should always be in writing. Never accept a verbal guarantee.

Then there is the used car sold "as is," and on such a car the dealer offers no warranty as to its condition. He assumes no liability after the car is sold, although he may have said, "I guarantee it to be in good condition." The "as is" clause may be in small type in the contract and hence unnoticed by the purchaser. *Accept no verbal guarantees, and read every word of your contract!*

If you do business with a reliable dealer, he will provide you with the name of the former owner and you can call him to learn how the car was used, the amount of mileage on it, and why he decided to sell or trade it in.

The odometer, which registers the miles

a car has traveled, may have been turned back to zero. This does not indicate that any deceit has been intended, for in some states this is required by law, and elsewhere dealers consider the mileage record undependable and set back the odometer so they do not have to make any representation concerning it. How the car was used and the purpose for which it was used are more important than the mileage registered.

LOOK IT OVER CAREFULLY

You should always examine a used car carefully before buying. If possible, have it checked over by a mechanic employed by yourself. You will find that the cost of such professional service is usually saved in the final accounting.

But if you decide to make your own examination, here are some things to look for:

1. The general appearance of the car may give you a good idea as to its previous use and care. If there are seat covers, look under-

CHECK A USED CAR CAREFULLY

Fender dents may indicate damage.

Check tires for wear.

Test the motor.

Check alignment of frame.

neath to see if the upholstery is worn or dirty. If worn, you can assume the car has had hard usage. If dirty, it may indicate neglect on the part of the previous owner—neglect which may have extended to the mechanical parts. Determine if the car has its original paint. This might be revealed on the inside edges of the doors, and under the fenders where traces of the old paint may show.

2. Look for tears and leakage in convertible fabric tops, and see if the tops operate properly. The front floor boards and foot pedals will tell something of the kind of treatment the car has had. Door catches and snubbers should be examined carefully. Lights, horn, spare tire, and tool kit should be checked.

3. Go over the fenders. Dents and repairs on fenders are not unusual in used cars, but if there is an outward indication of serious damage, look beneath for a better idea of how bad the damage was. A new fender should be viewed with suspicion. The car may have been in an accident and the old fender so badly damaged it could not be repaired.

4. Look carefully at the tires. Uneven or wavy wear may mean loose wheels or improper alignment. It the tires look new in relation to the car, it may be an indication that the car has traveled a considerable number of miles and that the old, worn-out tires have been replaced.

5. Check the instrument panel while the engine is running to see that the battery is charging, that the oil gauge shows pressure, and that the gas gauge works properly. The battery should turn the engine over easily and the motor should respond at once. If the motor "knocks," there may be a poor valve adjustment, loose bearings, worn pistons, carbon, or the spark may be advanced too far. If the motor misses or skips there may be trouble in the distributor or spark plugs.

6. While the engine is running, see if the exhaust pipe emits a bluish, heavy oil smoke. This may indicate worn pistons or rings. A heavy black smoke means the car is burning too rich a gas mixture and the carburetor needs adjusting.

7. When the motor has run for a time, take a look at the gaskets, water pump, hose, and

radiator to see if there is any sign of water leakage.

8. Check the car's steering gear and king-pins for looseness and wheel alignment. Too much play in the steering wheel could mean loose steering connections.

9. Also check the axle, chassis, and engine block for cracks or welding. See that the brakes are adjusted properly. The foot brake pedal should not push down more than two inches from the floor.

10. Check the alignment of the wheels. This can be judged to some extent by the wear of the tires.

11. Jack up one of the rear wheels. Set the gear shift in high gear, with the motor not running. Jerk the rear wheel from side to side to determine the amount of play. If the play is more than three inches, it indicates excessive wear in the differential or universal joints. Shift to low gear and also reverse gear and test the transmission in the same way for looseness.

12. Be certain the frame is not bent or twisted. A car badly out of line may be detected by having someone watch it front and rear as it is driven on a straight road. The rear wheels should follow the front wheels in a straight line.

13. A car that has been in a bad wreck usually is a poor bargain and may later prove dangerous. Examine the frame by looking down the sides of the car to see whether they are straight, or have been straightened.

14. In shopping for a used car, look out for repainted taxicabs which are offered as cars previously privately owned. Most taxi-cabs are four-door sedans. They usually have been turned in after intensive, hard usage. There are several ways to detect a former taxicab. One is to stand so the light falls on the side, for thus you may be able to detect the outline of the taxicab name under the new paint. Another is to examine the dash and toe boards, because taxicabs have different holes than are found in regular cars.

Good secondhand cars can often be found in former fleet, lease, or rental cars. Such cars usually are purchased in numbers by business firms for use by officials or employees and for rental purposes. While they often are driven by many different persons and run up more mileage in a year than a privately owned car, they frequently are traded in every year, or after registering a certain number of miles. While some are in poor shape by this time, many receive regular care and servicing and may be good values.

A reliable dealer usually will not object to your taking a car out for a driving test. It is then that you can determine the good and bad points of the car. However, if you are asked to sign a paper before you take the car out, be certain it is not a sales contract. Read it carefully before signing. If a deposit is asked, get a receipt which clearly states that your money will be refunded if you are not satisfied.

In buying a used car do not make up your mind in a hurry. Shop around. The thought that should always be in your mind is: "I will not buy a used car if I can find a new one at the same price which suits my needs."

POLICY NO. 19596X

THE FINANCIAL SIDE OF OWNING A CAR

CHAPTER **12**

WHEN you become the owner of a car, you will find yourself concerned with various financial problems in addition to financing the purchase price. There is the matter of insurance—what kinds will you need, and how much should you carry? There is also the matter of income tax deductions connected with your car. What deductible expenses will you be able to claim, and how can you keep track of these expenses for tax purposes? These are important matters to every car owner, and you should spend some time in learning to understand them.

THE PENALTY OF YOUTHFUL CARELESSNESS

If all young drivers in the country got together and made a solemn pledge to drive more carefully and carried out this pledge, insurance rates for each car owner under twenty-five years of age would be much lower. Very much lower. As it is, and because insurance companies base their rates on the number and severity of insurance claims in certain age groups, the male driver under twenty-five pays the highest premium.

For instance: A driver over twenty-five driving a pleasure car may pay a total of $144 annually for coverage—including collision insurance with a $50 deductible clause; comprehensive (fire and theft); property damage up to $5,000; and bodily injury of $10,000 per person and $20,000 per accident.

But a driver under twenty-five may pay a total of $367.40 for the same coverage!

The costs are classified thus:

For collision ($50 deductible) & comprehensive $132.00
For property damage $5,000 . . . . 65.00
For bodily injury $10,000 & $20,000 . . 170.40

The types and amounts of insurance listed above are considered normal coverage. These amounts can, of course, be increased.

COLLISION AND "COMPREHENSIVE"

Collision insurance helps pay the cost for damage to your car if you run into another car. (If another car hits you, the driver of that car is liable for the damage to your car.) Few companies will sell you a collision insurance policy without at least a "$50 deductible" clause. This means you pay for the first $50 worth of damage and the insurance company pays for the balance.

If you consider yourself to be a safe driver and unlikely to run into another car because of carelessness, the chances are your collision losses usually will not amount to more than $50. You might therefore consider a $100 or even a $250 deductible clause, which would give you a lower rate. This means you have to pay the first $100 or the first $250. Many drivers drop collision insurance entirely after their car becomes two or three years old.

The so-called "comprehensive" policy pays for direct or accidental loss of, or damage to your car from, fire or theft, glass breakage, vandalism, wind, storm, hail, flood—and other causes as listed in your policy.

WATCH OUT FOR LIABILITY

But liability insurance is another matter. This is vitally important since it protects you, as owner of the car, against claims of another person for injury or damage resulting from an accident caused by your car.

The two main parts of liability insurance cover *bodily injury* and *property damage*. Claims for bodily injury to another person or persons often run into thousands of dollars. Lawsuits in which the claimants are awarded from $50,000 to $100,000 are not unusual.

Such a risk is much more serious than loss of your car because it has NO TOP LIMIT. Everything you can call your own that is an asset is at stake. So bear down on liability insurance. Take all you can afford—and certainly all the law requires.

As your protection goes up, the cost per $1,000 coverage of such insurance goes down. Many drivers carry $25,000 or more for injury to one person, and $50,000 or more for any one accident. This "25 & 50" costs just 37 per cent more than "5 & 10"; that is, $5,000 and $10,000.

INSURANCE COMPANIES

There are more than 600 companies that will insure your car. These include stock companies, which are owned by stockholders who have invested their money to afford greater security to the policyholder; mutual companies, where policyholders are owners and share in both profits and losses of the company; and reciprocals, which are organizations such as motor clubs, formed to spread the risks among the policyholders.

You can save money by selecting your insurance company wisely, but be sure it is a reputable concern. Sometimes car dealers serve as agents for various insurance companies and may try to pressure you into doing business with the company they represent,

WHAT YOUR CAR INSURANCE COVERS

Collision damage (to you).

Fire and theft, and other losses.

Property damage (to others).

Bodily injury (to others).

but you are not obliged to do so. You will be better satisfied if you shop around a bit first and compare rates before deciding. There are many reputable insurance companies, as well as banks, that will be glad to advise you as to your insurance needs.

TAX DEDUCTIONS

If you are under twenty-one, and if you are not working, the chances are your tax deductions will be taken care of by your father. He will deduct from his income tax certain recognized deductible expenses in connection with your car, as well as his own. But if you are earning any money, even while living at home, you will have to make out an income tax return, and if you use your car in connection with your job you are entitled to make certain deductions for business expenses.

First, let us look at tax deductions *not* connected with business expense. When the car is purchased, there are some tax deductible items right on the bill of sale. These include any sales tax paid to the state, county, or city, and fees for registration—but not for title or safety inspection.

Under this same head you (or your father) can deduct the annual registration fee for license plates, city or county tax (stickers), driver's license fee, and property tax on the car. All such deductions are listed on the income tax return as "Taxes Paid."

If the car was purchased through a finance company, all finance charges paid each month on the loan can be deducted as "Interest Paid."

Keep a record throughout the year of all gasoline and oil purchases. The state tax and the local sales tax on these can be deducted. The federal tax is *not* deductible.

If during the taxable year your car has been damaged in an accident or there has been a loss by theft, any expenses not paid by your insurance company are deductible. Most policies covering collision contain a $50 (or more) deductible clause. This $50 can be deducted as a loss on your income tax return.

THE YOUNG BUSINESSMAN

If your car is used part time for business, keep a careful record of the time it is so used and the mileage it runs up. Regular operating costs, in addition to the taxes, interest, and casualty losses, can be deducted from your income tax return since these operating costs are incurred in producing income.

A vehicle schedule, listing date of purchase of your car, or date of sale or trade, and amounts involved in each instance, as well as a record of mileage and repairs, should be kept. Gas and oil, lubrication, title fees, maintenance, repairs, tires, parking fees, and insurance are all deductible during the time business mileage was built up.

HOW TO FIGURE DEPRECIATION

The next thing, and a highly important one, is figuring the depreciation on your car. Of course, if it is used solely for business during the entire year, the total depreciation, calculated as the cost of replacing this used-up portion of your car, can be deducted. But in part-time operation for business purposes, only the percentage of total time or mileage used for business is the ratio on which you can calculate deductible depreciation.

Each car has a basic salvage value of around 20 per cent of its cost, depending upon the car use. Let us consider a car which cost $3,000. Its salvage value would be $600.

YEARLY AUTOMOBILE EXPENSE RECORD

Month	Speedometer reading at beginning of month	Gasoline		Oil		Lubri-cation	Tires	Main-tenance	Repairs	Miscel-laneous
		No. of Gallons	Total Cost	No. of Quarts	Total Cost					
Jan.										
Feb.										
March										
April										
May										
June										
July										
Aug.										
Sept.										
Oct.										
Nov										

For yearly automobile costs, use a chart like the one above for recording monthly automobile expenses. Enter all figures each month. At the end of the year, you will know exactly how much to allow for car expenses in your money management plan.

From *Money Management, Your Automobile Dollar.* © by Household Finance Corp.

This leaves $2,400 in "depreciable assets," and should you trade for a new car each three years, you would be entitled to charge $800 depreciation each year as a part of operating costs.

The dealer's trade-in allowance on your old car will increase or decrease depreciation. It might be that you have deducted too little or too much each year during your ownership. However, this matter is one best handled by a visit to your local Internal Revenue Office or your own tax accountant.

BUSINESS USE VS. PLEASURE

In establishing the percentage of time you drive a car for business and for pleasure, take the total mileage for the year. Add up your business mileage from the records you have kept and divide by the total mileage. This gives you the percentage for business use. Perhaps you have driven a total of 10,000 miles during the year, and your business mileage is 2,500. Divide the total mileage into the business mileage, and you would find you used the car 25 per cent of the time for business.

In such a case you are entitled to deduct 25 per cent of (1) the cost of gasoline and oil, (2) title and auto inspection fees, (3) lubri-cation, repairs, and washing, (4) tires and supplies, (5) garage and parking fees, (6) insurance, and (7) depreciation.

IT'S NOT THE ORIGINAL COST—

It's the upkeep.

So have your pencil and notebook handy at all times and jot down every item of expense connected with your car.

This record will not only come in handy for reference at the end of the year—showing how much mileage you get per gallon of gas, how much it costs to drive a mile in your car, and providing data for your income tax report—but it will also enable you to budget your expenses for the following year.

Besides depreciation, which is always with you, there are *fixed costs* and *flexible expenses*, covering many miscellaneous items.

Fixed costs include expenses throughout the year such as insurance, license fees, garage rent, and if the car has not been paid for, the installment payments.

Flexible expenses include such items as gasoline, oil, tires, maintenance, and miscellaneous things such as polishing, parking fees, inspections, tolls, antifreeze, etc., connected with the operation of your car.

Put down everything.

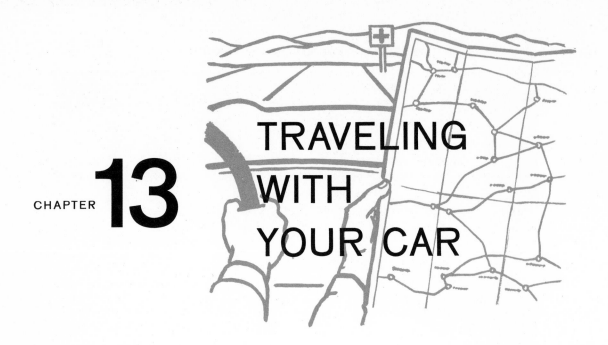

CHAPTER 13

TRAVELING WITH YOUR CAR

THE real joy of driving comes when you hit the open road. Your car is in tiptop order, engine tuned and functioning perfectly, with a fresh oil change and grease job, tires checked and properly inflated, windows open to the balmy air, sun shining and scenery beautiful. These are ideal conditions. There will be exceptions, of course.

THE OPEN ROAD

It is possible to drive by interlocking toll systems the thousand miles between Chicago and Boston without encountering a single stop light! Some day such a trip will be possible from coast to coast, or from Canada to the Gulf of Mexico.

While traffic regulations vary slightly in different states, there is no differentiation in regard to the major violations. You cannot plead ignorance of the law in any state when driving under the influence of liquor or narcotics, passing on a hill, or parking your car on a highway. Speed regulations are also basically the same throughout the fifty states. To play safe, drive with traffic, letting those familiar with the local speed laws regulate your own speed.

PLANNING YOUR TRIP

Planning your vacation or outing by automobile is in itself exciting. With a general idea in mind of the interesting places you wish to visit, go to your local library and learn as much as you can about what you hope to see. Write or visit a leading oil company or motor club and obtain road maps marked to show the most direct route, or the "scenic" route, whichever you prefer. Note especially the total mileage and calculate on driving from 300 to 400 miles a day. Give yourself plenty of time. You will have more fun and it will prove cheaper.

Sometimes you may wish to go "vagabonding," just starting out with no particular destination in mind, traveling the so-called "off-beat" roads, and visiting the "tourist-free" communities. This can often be fun, but such a trip requires a certain amount of preparation, too.

MAP READING

Good maps are essential for cross-country driving. Individual state maps can be obtained at your motor club or at a gas station. Best of all is a road atlas which will provide not only roads and highways in all states, but also tables showing distances between major cities, street layouts in the larger cities, and federal requirements for entering and leaving Canada and Mexico.

Learn to "read" your maps. Study them carefully. Pay special attention to the "Legend" shown in one corner of the map. This legend will indicate a scale of miles, show symbols and markings, and explain the types of roads on the map. Distances between towns and cities are imprinted on the map itself, alongside the connecting road or highway.

Symbols will indicate whether a road is paved, hard-surfaced, graded earth, or what. National routes are marked by the letters "U.S." and designated by numbers within a shield on the route itself. State numbers are enclosed in a circle.

Cities and towns shown on a road map usually can be found listed alphabetically on the back of the map. They are keyed by num-

bers and letters. On the map itself the numbers most often are at the top of the map and the letters on the side. If a certain place is indicated in the index as A-6, for instance, locate the letter A and the numeral 6, then project the lines from each and about where they intersect will be found the city or town. Many maps show places of interest along a route.

If driving alone, never attempt to consult a map while the car is in motion. Wait until you can safely stop and then look at your map.

WHERE TO EAT

When in doubt as to where to stop for a quick meal, don't overlook the often-satirized advice, "It has to be good—all the truck drivers eat there." Such places—usually roadside diners—are satisfactory when patronized by local as well as transient trade. When you

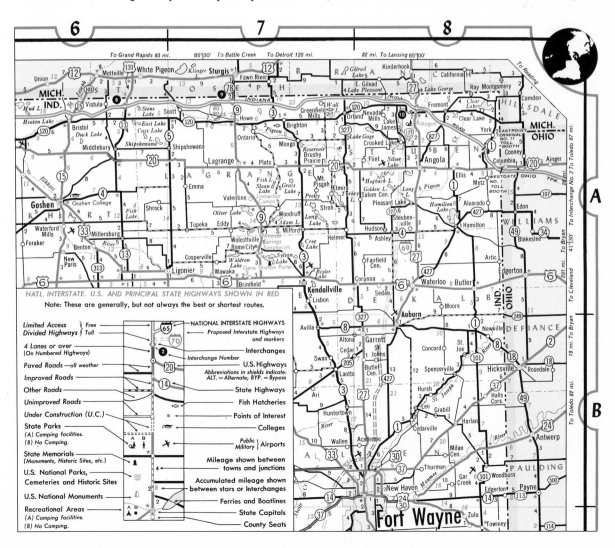

want a more formal meal, a gas station attendant or other local citizen can usually answer your question as to "Where is the best restaurant in town?"

There are also available lists of "recommended" eating places prepared by touring agencies or travel experts. These usually indicate the price range of the restaurants in the community as well as their specialities as to food or service. Well-known chain restaurants and state-franchised eating places on turnpikes offer dependable and uniform menus.

A good rule is to "live off the land," so to speak. Eat the food characteristic of the area. Seafood might be good in New England, for instance, and bad in the Middle West. Almost every region has certain specialties you will enjoy.

WHERE TO SLEEP

There are travel guides listing recommended motels as well as eating places, but it is difficult to keep the information in them up to date. Look at the room offered you before you sign the register, and be satisfied. Bad motels are apt to charge just as much as good ones. Some of the best motels are affiliated with a national organization and have an identifying insignia.

It is a good policy to make your reservations ahead. If you are satisfied with the accommodations at the place you are staying, the manager possibly can make a reservation for you at a motel equally good at your next stop.

"Tourist homes," and even private residences offering rooms, are not to be scorned. They may be more comfortable and cheaper than a motel room, particularly in smaller communities.

TRAVEL TIPS

If you want to travel with a carefree mind, be sure your car has a complete checkup before you start on any long trip. Have the tires and brakes inspected carefully, see that the battery is in good condition, and take care of any necessary repairs or replacements before you leave home.

Then when on the road, have the oil changed every 1,000 miles—which means, at average driving, about every three to four days. (This does not, of course, apply to cars where oil changes are unnecessary for 5,000 miles or "lube jobs" for 30,000 miles.) If you travel as far as 6,000 miles, get an engine tune-up.

Watch your tires. Pressure should be checked each morning before starting out, when the tires are cool. Pressure should remain consistent.

Plan well ahead for gasoline stops. Some places close on certain holidays and on Sundays. You cannot afford to run out of gas miles between gasoline stations. Pay attention to the slightest grind or minor noise and have it checked and remedied as quickly as possible. It may develop into a major problem.

By careful planning your trip can be pleasant—so, Happy Wheeling!

GOOD DRIVING QUIZ

1. When approaching a traffic signal showing a **green** light, you should:
   A. Speed up so that you can reach the intersection before a red light appears.
   B. Proceed, but with regard for the safety of others.
   C. Stop and wait for the red light.

2. In heavy traffic on a rural highway, it is best to:
   A. Drive at the speed of other traffic provided the traffic is moving below the posted speed limit.
   B. Drive slowly on the extreme right.
   C. Pass cars until you find an open space ahead.

3. When approaching a traffic signal showing a **flashing** yellow light, you should:
   A. Slow down and proceed with caution.
   B. Proceed, you have the right of way.
   C. Come to a full stop and proceed when safe.

4. You are driving on a snow-covered road and have to make a stop rather quickly. The best way to do this is to:
   A. Turn off the ignition switch and apply the hand brake.
   B. Pump the brake pedal gently to avoid locking the wheels.
   C. Slam the brakes on hard.

5. A good driver, suddenly finding that the foot brakes are not working, will try to control the car for stopping by:
   A. Turning off the ignition switch.
   B. Driving on the shoulder of the road to slow the car.
   C. Pulling back the hand brake, then shifting into second gear.

6. When parking parallel to the right edge of a roadway where there is no curb, it is best to:
   A. Leave the front wheels turned toward the edge of the road.
   B. Leave the front wheels turned toward the center of the road.
   C. Keep the front wheels pointed straight ahead.

7. The most frequent type of traffic accident fatality in urban areas occurs when cars collide with
   A. Pedestrians   C. Fixed objects
   B. Other cars   D. Bicycles

8. In driving around a curve, you should:
   A. Speed up at the beginning of the curve, then apply brakes if necessary.
   B. Slow down before reaching the curve, depress the clutch and coast around the curve.
   C. Slow down before reaching the curve, start around at a safe speed, then speed up slightly just before reaching the straightaway.

9. When meeting a car with glaring headlights, the driver should:
   A. Watch the right side of the road.
   B. Turn on his own bright lights.
   C. Watch the center line of the road.

10. If a blowout occurs on the right front tire, the driver should:
    A. Jam on the brakes.
    B. Steer in a straight line and release the gas pedal.
    C. Steer sharply to the left.

11. Your car has entered an intersection when you notice a driver bluffing his way forward from a side street into your path. You should:
    A. Pretend not to see him so he will back up to his correct position.
    B. Swerve to your left and pass him to avoid an accident.
    C. Slow down and let him go ahead.

12. When the right front wheel of your car slips off the edge of the pavement you should:
    A. Apply brakes quickly in order to keep from going into the ditch.
    B. Turn back onto the pavement before the car has lost speed.
    C. Slow down gradually until you can steer back onto the pavement at a convenient place.

13. You are driving on a straight stretch of slippery road with no approaching vehicles. The rear of your car starts to skid to your left. Which of the following steps should you take?
    A. Apply the brakes hard to stop before sliding off the road.
    B. Put the clutch pedal down and pump the brakes.
    C. Release the gas pedal slowly and turn the front wheels to your left.

ANSWERS: 1. B, 2. A, 3. A, 4. B, 5. C, 6. A, 7. B, 8. C, 9. A, 10. B, 11. C, 12. C, 13. C.

Courtesy of The National Safety Council

INDEX

PRINTED IN U.S.A.